Behind the Wheel

A mother's journal of a year on the road

Wendy Swart Grossman

Ruby Beech Press

Boston • London

Ruby Beech Press

Brookline, MA 02446

Visit our Web site at www.familyadventureyear.com

Cover design: Steve Amarillo, Urban Design, LLC

Cover photos: Jupiterimages / Comstock / Thinkstock and Hemera /
Thinkstock

ISBN: 978-0615473581

Table of Contents

Section IV – Going Home

A word of thanks...

Thank you to our wonderful supportive parents, brothers, sister-in-laws, aunts, uncles, cousins and friends who have listened to us, supported us, fed us and shared their washers and dryers with us. Your love and encouragement kept us from ending up on the side of the road as opposed to on it.

Thank you to all the librarians we met as we used your libraries as our classrooms across the US and Canada. Your brilliance and patience astounds us.

Thank you to all the incredible Park Rangers with the National Park Service who were our teachers and guides. Your passion and knowledge awakened our senses.

Thank you to our new and old friends in Boston and Brookline who have caught us safely.

Thank you Josh and Simon for your generosity in letting me tell a part of the story.

And, of course, thank you Evan. My partner in parenthood, adventure, and life. Where next, baby?

Go confidently in the direction of your dreams.
Live the life you have imagined.
Henry David Thoreau

Be aware when an opportunity arises and don't be
afraid to jump . . . but not out the window.
Wendy Swart Grossman

The road trip has given new meaning to the term
'Two Bar Town'.
Evan Grossman
[commenting on Blackberry coverage across America]

You have ruined my life. All my friends are 4,000
miles away and we live in an RV.
Joshua M. Grossman

Our RV may be small
but the world is our garden.
Simon David Ace Swart Grossman

Introduction

I don't like being woken up in the middle of the night—especially by a bunch of drunks. But when you are sleeping in the cheap seats on the 18-hour train ride from Thompson to Churchill, Manitoba, you don't get to choose your fellow passengers. So when six stinky drunks barged through our train car at 2:00 A.M. talking wildly about the end of the world, not only was I not pleased, I also was getting ready to morph into Mom-zilla.

Yes, this is a story about our adventure in an RV—but you can't drive to Churchill, Manitoba. The road ends in Thompson. So, we parked the RV for a week at McCreedy Campground on the north side of Thompson and hopped aboard the slowest express train this side of the tundra. There are three reasons people go to Churchill: the aurora borealis, beluga whales, and polar bears. We were going for the polar bears.

In those early morning hours, we were camped out at the far end of the train car, so I had a bit of time to compose myself as our inebriated gentlemen callers weaved their way past the lovely young French women we had talked with earlier that evening. Marie Claire was also awake and we exchanged a quick, knowing, 2:00 A.M. eye roll that said in both French and English, "Don't you hate it when you are almost to the arctic tundra and you get woken up by smelly drunk guys?"

I took inventory. Seven-year-old Simon was cuddled up between me and the window, safe and snug. My husband, Evan, and twelve-year-old Josh were in the two seats behind us. Evan was against the window, snoring and sound asleep. Josh, however, was sleeping on the aisle, next to the sliding door. His arm was flopping off the side of the seat, which left him exposed to the drunken prophets now just a few seats away.

When Evan and I were planning this adventure on the road, we talked about how this trip would be a great opportunity for our kids to confront problems that they just wouldn't have in their admittedly sheltered life. What a gift it would be to give our kids the chance to learn how to be creative problem solvers. But this scenario really wasn't what I had in mind.

Josh woke up just as one of the guys was hovering over him, yelling in his face with his hairy breath. "2012. Get ready people. We are all going to F***ing DIE." Josh, in a sleepy voice, quietly retorted, "Oh, the Mayan Prophecy—I don't believe it." And he rolled over and went back to sleep as the drunks stumbled off the train at the next stop and disappeared into a dark, remote town in the middle of nowhere.

I absolutely hate the pithy expression "That which doesn't kill you makes you stronger." I hate even more that it is true. Taking time off and traveling the country is a dream that many people have. Being able to take that time to bond with your kids while in the lap of incredible beauty, have shared experiences, and connect in ways you never realized . . . it is all so romantic. It is also incredibly lonely, isolating, boring, nerve-wracking, and butt numbing.

Our RV trip was borne less out of a grand life plan and never-ending thirst for adventure and more out of adversity. In January 2009, Evan's position at his software company was changing and it was time for him to move on. We had been relocated to London, England, six years earlier and had enjoyed an amazing run of expatriate adventures around Europe with the kids. Now, since my career as a consultant to nonprofits was not lucrative enough to foot the bills, it seemed like this was the right time to move back to the U.S.A. Unfortunately, this was all playing out during the worst economic downturn since the Great Depression.

When I told my friend Nikola, a fellow adventurer, expat, traveler, and mother, that we would be selling our house and moving back to the U.S., she exclaimed, "What a gift! What an opportunity!" As soon as the words were out of her mouth I knew exactly what she meant, and I knew Evan would as well. Our house was sold, his company was paying to have all our stuff shipped back to the U.S., and he had six months of severance pay. If we lived close to the bone we could eke out a year of living and a lifetime of memories.

And hopefully, by the time we were ready to settle down, the worst of the economic downturn would be behind us and we would be able to find jobs.

That evening Evan and I had a secret conference out of earshot of the boys. As soon as I told him about my conversation with Nikola, he was on it like gum to the sole of a sneaker on a hot summer day. Evan and I make a scary pair. I am the ideas gal and he is the make-it-happen guy. We thought, *Why not take this great opportunity to travel the U.S. in an RV, reconnect with friends and family, and introduce the kids to the land of their birth?* Within a week Evan had the family website set up (www.familyadventureyear.com) and was researching RVs. Over the ensuing months we hammered out the details—from movers, storage facilities, homeschooling, and health care to RV insurance, technology on the road, U.S. National Park Junior Ranger programs, and expected snowfall in the Grand Canyon.

More important, we tried to figure out what it was we wanted to do with our time on the road together as a family. It wasn't going to be a yearlong vacation but a yearlong adventure. Our budget wouldn't allow for restaurants, swimming with dolphins, or drinking Pina Coladas by the pool. We would be teaching school, wallowing in nature, going to Laundromats, working and playing together, and hopefully making memories that we as a family would be able to draw on and use as a touchstone for the rest of our lives.

Before we set out Evan and I had a ton of hopes, ideas, and dreams about what this transformative adventure would mean. And being the neurotic Virgo list maker I am, here they are:

Seven Goals for the Trip

1. We want to pull our sheltered kids out of their bubble of privilege and have them confront real problems so that as they grow up they will be creative problem solvers.

2. We want to use this time to reimagine and redefine ourselves as a family and our relationships with one another. And finally get to the bottom of that age-old question: Is our family a democracy or a benevolent dictatorship?

3. We can't predict when an opportunity for a fabulous conversation will happen with our kids, but we want to be there when it arises. With this year of open time lines and time on our hands, the odds will be in our favor.

4. We want to recalibrate our boys' values. After leading a privileged life in London, we see that there has been nothing more disturbing than hearing our kids ask, "How many stars is this hotel?" or worse yet, when asked to clean their rooms, "But that's what the cleaning lady is supposed to do." Living in a shared space of 239 square feet a lot more will be expected of them. We will also have Josh, as a sixth grader, take the role of our Chief Financial Officer (CFO) so he can appreciate how quickly a dollar can fly out of a clenched fist.

5. We want to reacquaint ourselves with American culture and terrain, introduce our sons to their native country, and see the U.S. through their eyes. While our boys are very familiar with traveling they have little idea of distance. What does it feel like to drive 1,000 miles? How are the states connected? Airplanes are more like transporter rooms but by living with maps and having to be aware of local weather patterns, gas stations, and safe places to camp, we will all need to be awake and involved for the trip.

6. We want to reclaim that feeling of reckless abandon that abandoned us once I was about seven months pregnant with our first child.

7. We want to show our kids we can be adventurous as a family and roll with the punches. We are making this uncertain time of having no job in a horrible economy into an opportunity—putting "when life gives you lemons, make lemonade" into practice.

But in all the excitement of planning the adventure I had forgotten the obvious. I was a menopausal woman and the mother of a preteen. I was the mother of a seven-year-old who loves imaginary play with other seven-year-olds. I was a woman who craves long chats and I was married to a wonderful—but quiet—man. I was prone to gain weight without regular exercise and access to fresh fruit and veggies. I tended to get ugly without my own space, and with only 239 square feet in the RV . . . do you see where this is going?

As the trip unfolded we realized we needed to strike a balance between our ridiculously lofty expectations and hopes for adventure with the ugly realities of life on the road. It quickly became clear that if we were going to be able to complete this trip we needed to make changes, go easy on ourselves, and just roll with it.

What follows are the blogs and notes I wrote throughout the twelve months before, during, and after the trip. They chronicle my slow descent into depravity in a way I hope you will find humorous, inspiring, and cautionary. And, if you're thinking you just may be crazy enough to throw caution to the wind, toss good sense out the window, and head off on a similar adventure, I encourage you to read through to the end so you can benefit from some of my mistakes.

And if you ever find yourself on an 18-hour overnight train ride to the arctic tundra, bring along extra pillows, earplugs, and a big old sense of humor.

Section I — London

Letter: The Road Forward
London

1 March 2009

Dear Friends and Family,

The stars are aligning and we are channeling our inner adventure spirit. With Evan leaving his job and Wendy's consulting gigs in the nonprofit world just not profitable enough, combined with the boys growing up faster than we would like—it is one of these rare opportunities to regroup, realign, and recharge.

We have loved living in London the past six years but our accents and loud voices can't deny we are Americans. Our kids don't remember living in the U.S. and, in some ways, neither do we. It is time to move home to the land of drive-through banks, Fourth of July parades, Trader Joe's, and smiling faces of friends and family.

But we aren't yet ready to settle down. We are pulling the kids out of school for the 2009/2010 school year and hitting the road. When else will we have this chance? The boys are at fabulous ages where they will remember the adventures, read their own chapter books, and write their own journals. And Josh is strong enough to carry a full-size suitcase . . . with wheels of course! Yet they aren't old enough to be too embarrassed to be seen with their parents.

Most sailors know that sometimes it's better to ride out a storm at sea, and rather than trying to settle down in the midst of the greatest financial crisis in 80 years, why not put the cash in the bank, resist taking on any new debt, and have some adventures in the process? We have to move anyway, all our stuff will be in storage, and we won't own a house. Is this irresponsible or is this just taking advantage of an opportunity?

Party on, Garth!

Enough with the justifications! This is an adventure on many fronts:

1. Explore the U.S.: visit Washington, D.C., and Philadelphia; follow Lewis and Clark's trail; hike in national parks; compare the circumferences of the largest ball of twine in Cawker City, Kansas, to the one in Darwin, Minnesota; investigate baseball stadiums and Laundromats;

2. Physical well-being: biking and hiking;

3. Community service: we are looking for a charity to work with in a meaningful way;

4. Family history and genealogy: hoping to spend time collecting stories and videotaping family lore;

5. Our own family-of-four dynamics: are we a democracy or benevolent dictatorship?

An RV is in our future! Needless to say we will be blogging, Facebooking, journaling, parking in your driveway, and mooching off your hospitality.

Happy trails to you, our friends!

Out of Body Experience

London

4 March 2009

March Fourth/Forth. I love this day—so full of possibilities. A great day to make things happen, push forward agendas, and get moving.

With that said, I haven't made any progress on the moving front today. In fact, all I have done the last week is wander around the house putting things away in preparation for potential house buyers. People come to look at a house that's for sale wanting to imagine *themselves* living there. They don't want to see the birthday party invitations on the fridge, the stupid postcard collection on the cork board, the book choices of the present occupiers next to the beds or—god forbid—the worn-down toothbrushes next to the bathroom sink. We are not selling ourselves— merely the vessel we live in. Save the interesting tidbits for the dinner parties, please.

But today the boys come home at 3:30 P.M. and then it is time for homework, haircuts, and dinner. The first people coming to look at the house at 5:30 and the next group at 6:00 might just have to deal with a bit of our reality. Perhaps we will save viola practice for after dinner.

It is interesting to hear the reactions of the potential buyers as they walk through the house. First there's usually the line about the master bedroom being too small. (Come on, man! There is room for a queen-size bed, two nightstands, and a bookshelf—what else do people do in their bedrooms? Never mind . . . strike that.) Second, many people have trouble with the fact that our garden backs up against the WORLD FAMOUS HOOP LANE CREMATORIUM AND MEMORIAL GARDENS.

Sigmund Freud and Anna Pavlova were both cremated there, for goodness sake. This is a shrine, and they should be so lucky! The Memorial Gardens are beautiful, and the view from our bedroom is spectacular: the gardens, the poplars, the open fields. Clearly these people have issues with death.

I have also been very busy eating many little snacks of varying degrees of healthiness and writing emails.

In reality, I have the attention span of a gnat. I am so overwhelmed with the Holy Trinity of Emotions: (1) profound sadness for leaving London; (2) terror of not knowing where we are going and where we will end up; and (3) excitement for the unknown and all the adventures that it holds in store for us.

I feel as if I am watching myself from the ceiling, and man oh man, am I ever boring.

To quote Simon, *"I feel like this (whole trip) isn't happening to me."*

Behind the Wheel

What is so weird is that when my brother Martin was tragically killed in a car accident in August of 1988, I also felt this way—like I was watching myself go through the motions from above.

That summer I was living in Dallas, Texas, with a lovely Democrat who had graciously donated her guest bedroom so I could live for free while I worked with the coordinated campaign led by Congressman Martin Frost's office for the election of Mike Dukakis and Lloyd Bentsen for President and Vice President.

At that point, I had been on the road for close to a year organizing various congressional districts, from the cornfields of Kansas to the beer-drinking college town of Stevens Point, Wisconsin, to the dying coal town of Steubenville, Ohio. I arrived in Dallas for the general election and in August things were looking like we still might have a chance.

Jennifer, my hostess, was a lawyer and a brilliant one at that, with a judgeship under her belt, a quiet yet mighty forcefulness to her voice, a dry wit, an artistic bent, and her heart in the right place. Each morning she went off to her office and I went to mine and rarely would I see her. Then one Tuesday afternoon she was in the campaign office. This wasn't all that rare and usually it meant something fun—a surprise check-in or a quick bite for lunch—so while I was surprised to see her, I was also excited. She was like an older sister and was serious about the role of watching over her 26-year-old charge. But that Tuesday was different. She came to tell me about my brother. She hardly knew me. My mom had called her and asked her to tell me in person because my mom wanted to make sure I wasn't alone.

Poor Jennifer, to have to be the one to tell me of my brother's death.

But as soon as she told me I immediately felt a rush of noise in my ears that wouldn't go away for months. As I look back on it now, I am on the ceiling watching myself on the floor looking up at Jennifer, searching her face. Wondering how a woman whom I had known for less than a month could say the name of my brother, whom she had never met. And now would never meet.

When Martin died at 28 he left behind my Korean sister-in-law, Sang, and their two children. My niece, Amy, was three and my nephew, Luke, was just one. Martin was a bit of a wild man. He was the kid in high school who never wore shoes. He was smarter than his teachers and he knew it. So did they. He jumped railroad cars and biked across the country more than once. He was the guy on skis who went straight down the mountain because turning was for wussies. Martin, like my boys, had red hair.

He wanted to be a millionaire by the time he was 30 to show my dad he could be successful without having gone to some fancy East Coast college—or college at all for that matter. And he did. He was already a millionaire when he died thanks to the highly exclusive and prestigious business of floor buffing and waxing.

Yesterday I got an email from Sang in response to our "Road Forward" letter telling all our friends and family that we would be moving from London to an RV for the year. Sang wrote to say that Martin had wanted to do a trip with her and Amy and Luke like the one we are planning.

Martin is going on this trip. He will be looking down at us as we are camping in the desert, protecting us as we drive over mountainous passages, and singing country western songs along with us as we listen to the radio. But he liked Merle Haggard and I prefer Hank Williams.

I guess life-changing events and out of body experiences are par for the course and this means I am a mere mortal.

Time to go put away the toothbrushes.

A Travel Addict

London

10 March 2009

Our RV trip is a natural extension of a long habit. For me, travel is like an addictive drug only it's legal. Once you do it, you want more. While you are on one trip, you start planning your next. While I never broke into people's houses to fund my next fix, I did spend most of my 20s and early 30s living with multiple roommates in questionably safe neighborhoods where the rent was cheap to save money for the next adventure.

At 19, I had my first experience as an exchange student at Chiang Mai University in Thailand. Visas, international borders, and malaria tablets. It was incredibly liberating and exciting with a sprinkle of scary thrown in. I love that combination. Then, when my grandfather died and left my brothers and me a little bit of money, I could have done the prudent thing and bought a car, or put it in the bank to start saving up for a house. Instead, I bought a blue Nishiki 18-speed road bike and lived on it while I rode from Athens, Greece, to London.

After that trip I thought I was done. I took a real job, one with health benefits that did not involve the words *may I take your order*. But then at 29 years old I relapsed, went off the wagon, and indulged my travel craving. I sold my 10-year-old Subaru hatchback, put my papasan chair from Pier 1 in storage, and spent six months wandering around West and East Africa, India, Nepal, and Australia.

Now I was done. I had "gotten it out of my system" once and for all. I had turned 30 standing on the equator in Kenya, slept on the Burkina Faso border, danced in a drumming circle, pulled through malaria in Mali, climbed an 18,000-foot peak in Nepal, travelled on the back of a motorcycle through New Delhi, and rode my bike through Australia.

But then I met Evan. A travel enabler.

We spent a wild holiday exploring Costa Rica on public buses and spent our honeymoon climbing Mount Kilimanjaro. The honeymoon was decidedly unromantic and included shared huts with flatulent Belgians, dead mice, and altitude sickness. But what is an adventure without adversity, challenges, altitude sickness, and assorted stomach viruses? Having that sense of accomplishment and being proud of yourself at the end of the day add to the richness to life.

When our first son was born we thought that was the end. Travel with a kid? No way. Too irresponsible. Too nerve-wracking. Too hard. Time to get life insurance. Save for college. Upgrade the kitchen. Have another kid. 2003 found us in Roswell, Georgia, with our two little red-headed boys. Evan worked at a software company and I was getting ready to go back to work in the nonprofit sector. We had moved to Georgia to follow a fabulous job for Evan, and while it was a great career move for him, it wasn't a good move for me. We made the mistake of moving into a faceless swim/tennis community and I stopped recognizing who I was. Conversations about window treatments, lawn care, and the next Bunco tournament just weren't doing it for me. I was going down fast—but not quietly. And if I was going down, I was taking Evan with me.

Then one evening Evan came home from work and asked, "What do you think about moving to London? There is an opportunity to set up the international office for my company." My world went from black-and-white to color again. The opportunity to move overseas on someone else's dime? When do we go? We sold the house in June and moved in August.

For almost six years now we have lived in the NW section of London raising our boys. Often I just shake my head in disbelief thinking that this is my life. How lucky I am. When I was single and 30 I never dreamed I would get married, have kids, own a house. And to have fallen in love with a guy who loves adventure, has good politics, makes a wonderful father, is brilliant, and shares nicely—this is all bonus!

And now onward in search of our next fix—in an RV. We won't need passports to travel between states, nor malaria tablets to protect us from the mosquitos. But I have a feeling we will need a big shot of a sense of humor.

Weird Al, Greg Brady, Me, and My Stuff

London

13 March 2009

With the impending move I look at all our stuff differently. Mostly my thought process is this:

How much will it cost to store this (fill in the blank with various household items) for a year?

Do we really need "it"? Can we eBay "it"?

When did *eBay* turn into a verb?

If we sell "it" for 5 quid now, will we need to buy some similar "it" when we eventually end up someplace?

And then there is Weird Al Yankovic's "eBay Song." My "its" will go alongside Smurf alarm clocks and William Shatner's toupee. I love Weird Al. I bet he doesn't love me. But that is ok.

I keep hearing about craigslist and how you can buy someone else's used "it" real cheap. Wouldn't it be cool if at the end of every block people could just put the things they want to get rid of in a box and other people could come along and take it? I guess Craig thought the same thing.

Who is Craig?

And then I start thinking about the big brother on the Brady Brunch and then I remember his name was Greg, not Craig. But now I am back in 1972 and the Friday night lineup with *The Brady Bunch, Room 222,* and *Love, American Style,* and how sexy it was for its time.

And then I think about London's page 3 in the daily papers and all the exposed breasts and the British love of a good Fancy Dress (costume) party along with men in drag yet folks on the whole are quite buttoned up in terms of daily interactions.

And then I think about all my wonderful friends and how it really takes a long time to make local British friends because they wonder if you are just passing through and whether or not it is really worth making the investment of time into a potential friend who is an expat because there is a chance you will be moving away. And I say to these potential British friends and neighbors, "That may be other expats you know but not me. Look. I am planting perennials in my garden." Oops. Now we are selling the house and the perennials along with it.

Someone else will be enjoying my garden. But that is ok. Because it still is adding enjoyment to someone. Maybe not me, not Greg Brady, nor Weird Al—but my neighbors on my wonderful street.

And I wonder how another day has slipped by and I have still yet to get anything done.

The Boys and the Obamas

London

21 March 2009

This following story has nothing to do with our upcoming RV trip but it certainly is helping us get excited for returning to the U.S. and the new chapter our country is writing!

Here is the back story: When Evan realized President Obama would be in London for the G20, he got in touch with his contact from the White House Office of Scheduling and Advance, whom he had worked with for the 2008 Presidential Inauguration at the White House. Evan offered his assistance, and much to his surprise, they took him up on it. For the past 10 days Evan has been working for the WH Office of Scheduling and Advance in charge of the motorcade.

He got to fly in a Chinook on Saturday on the dry run from the airport to the embassy, he got to measure the gate at Buckingham Palace to make sure the big U.S. car that was flown over would fit through (it wouldn't, so they switched cars), he brought in our fancy coffee maker to the advance office so the other staffers (mostly marines and 20-somethings who get paid nothing) could get a cup of coffee for free rather than paying 2 pounds a cup around the corner, he got tours for the kids of the cool cars and the embassy, and last night . . . well . . . then there was last night . . .

Behind the Wheel

The President was doing a meet-and-greet at the American School in a closed event for Embassy staff and their families. This is protocol so he can thank his employees who are working so hard abroad. Since Evan is a temporary employee of the White House, we were invited. There were about 1,000 people in the gym. The President and Mrs. Obama (she was wearing a brilliant yellow dress with black cardigan) arrived and he spoke for about 10 minutes, basically thanking all the career foreign service people for doing such an incredible job, being diplomats in all their dealings, for not much pay, and then he thanked them for bringing the children. It was about 9:15 in the evening at this point. He said he and Michelle were already missing their kids. But he reminded everyone that this is why we work so hard—for our kids. And to see them making connections and having experiences makes it all worthwhile.

We then had the incredible honor of being escorted to a private foyer to meet the President. There were also two groups of police and military officers who were having their photos taken as well.

Yesterday afternoon the boys and I discussed that there was a chance we could meet the President and how, since there was a chance, we needed to be prepared. We practiced "Hello, President Obama. It is an honor to meet you." And then we practiced questions . . . just in case they had an opportunity. I am still reeling and don't know how much I was really paying attention because mostly I was thinking, "OMG we are meeting the President. OMG we are meeting the President." (Luckily the boys were much better poised.) However, to the best of my recollection, this is how it went:

Pres (to Simon): Well hello, young man.
S: Hello, Mr. President. It is an honor to meet you.
P: And what is your name?
S: Simon.
P : And how old are you?
S: Seven and I have a question for you.
P: You do?
S: Do you know what the state fish of Hawaii is?
P (Big smile): Well, I used to know. Let me think . . . the humuhumu isn't it?
S: Well . . . it is the humuhumunukunukuapua'a.
Michelle: The what?
S: The humuhumunukunukuapua'a.
M: Can you say that again?
(lots of laughter and photos from paparazzi)
P: What a smart young man you are. How do you know that?
S: We are studying the ocean in school.

Josh: Hello, Mr. President. I am very honored to meet you.
P: Hello there, and what is your name?

J: Joshua Martin Swart Grossman, and I am in fifth grade here at the American School.

P: Nice to meet you.

J: I have a question for you as well, Mr. President.

P: Yes?

J: In fifth grade here at ASL the entire class is studying Africa, and my research is on conflict diamonds. I wonder if you could tell me what your position is on the conflict and any thoughts you may have?

P (Big smile, looking throughout the room): Well, nobody briefed me on this one! (Smiling at Josh and looking very thoughtful) But that deserves a thoughtful answer because it is such a horrible issue. As you know there are many countries in Africa and many of them are involved and lots of people are being exploited and hurt in the process. I believe that the countries must come together to get a hold of the situation and that people should be careful and make sure that if they are buying diamonds they are only coming from areas that are being respectful and legal in their diamond production.

At that point I made a stupid comment about buying only cubic zirconium diamonds, and we all got in position for the photo above.

At one point Michelle (can I call her Michelle?) commented that our boys are the same ages as their girls. How I wished I had mentioned that we would be coming through Washington, D.C., in the RV in a few months and maybe we could drop by, park the rig in the drive, and have a playdate.

Now that would be a story!

Flirting with Wife Swap

London

1 April 2009

Two years ago, Evan and I received an email from the minister of our Unitarian Church in Hampstead. He was forwarding a request from someone he thought was a documentary filmmaker. She appeared to be looking for families to interview regarding their beliefs and how they instilled religious values in their children and how religion is incorporated in their homes.

Being the chatty, questioning frustrated television personality that I am, I got in touch with the filmmaker. We had a fascinating conversation about religion in the U.K., value-based decision making, how to raise children to care about others, the various cultural issues that come up raising children abroad, and how we incorporate elements of both the Jewish and Christian faiths in our home. This was the basic 45-minute fun conversation with an interesting person who wanted to hear all about me and my family. I love talking about me and my family. No wonder I loved it.

And then we got down to the nitty-gritty.

She was working for a production company I had never heard of. Which isn't saying much, as I don't think I know the names of *any* production companies. And then I admitted I don't watch television aside from the children's channels. *Bob the Builder, Blue Peter,* and *Noddy* were not on her affiliate. She told me she was a producer for a program called *Wife Swap.*

That meant nothing to me other than what immediately came to mind, and the title was a little frightening. "Is this some sort of Adult Channel?" I asked. She mailed me some DVDs of the show.

The concept of the show is to take two very different families and swap the mothers for two weeks. The first week, the family lives under the existing rules but with the other mother. The second week, the other mother can change the rules so they are in line with her own thinking, morals, and neurotic obsessions. That is when the excitement starts.

Evan and I watched *Wife Swap.* The kids watched *Wife Swap.* Evan thought we should do it. Josh, then nine, was chomping at the bit to do it. "I will be famous!" he shouted.

Simon, then five, said, "No way! I can't be without you for two weeks."

Evan, my personal cheerleader, thought I would come across wonderfully. He suggested that I could use our 15 minutes of fame to show others what a fabulous job we are doing as parents and how others can incorporate similar values into their homes as well. Oh goodness. And what values would those be?

All I could imagine was me screaming and swearing at someone on national television. Then people on the street would point out our house to their friends: "That is where the obnoxious Americans who did *Wife Swap* live." Yes, we might be famous, but it would be for all the wrong reasons.

Then the producer called back, and called back, and called again. She was so smooth, so complimentary, so interested in having us on their show.

We decided to take it to the next step. They sent a camera crew out to see how we would look on camera.

We passed the test. "You are naturals! The camera loves you!" said the producer. Yes, we were ready for that close-up.

Now the pressure was really on. The phone calls continued. Could we do it next month? If not then, when? They claimed to have the perfect (undisclosed) family for us to swap with.

Luckily, we had a well-timed dinner with my brother and sister-in-law, who were also living in London, and some friends of theirs. Turns out the friend had worked at the same television production house, and she talked sense into us. We would have no control over anything. Whatever the most controversial argument, whenever someone lost it—that would be the five-second clip they would play over and over to get people interested in watching the program. I understand. It is all about increasing viewership, which translates into advertising dollars. Why would I knowingly throw myself into that sort of milieu? If we have a message we want to get out, then we can write a book and do it on our own terms.

The producer called again. This time I was ready and gave the firm I-really-mean-it-this-time NO.

With our upcoming RV adventure, I have thought about what it would be like to make this into a reality television show. Maybe we could sell this to someone. Maybe it would be lucrative enough so we could extend the adventure and do that Australia piece we just can't afford.

But why?

Again, all I can think about is all of us losing it and yelling obscenities at each other in the RV and never being able to get paid work again.

However, if *Good Morning America* would like to do a few interviews— we are available. We have been told that the camera loves us!

The Morality of the RV

London

18 April 2009

I just looked at the photos of the tent cities that are popping up around the U.S. The Modern Day Hoovervilles. The New Jack Cities.

And what are we doing? We are preparing to have an adventure year and I feel as if I am rubbing our good fortune in the faces of the have-nots. There are people living in garden sheds in Sacramento for God's sake! Who are we to go traipsing around looking for our own self-absorbed spiritual enlightenment? Alright, maybe it is not as self-indulgent as that, but I can see the self-absorbed aspects pretty clearly.

The other question staring me in the face when I saw those photos was: Why are we considering a community service opportunity in India when there are people who need our help in the U.S.? Is it too hard to volunteer at home and to see others in need in our own backyard? What are we running from?

When I worked for the Fund for Democratic Elections in South Africa—a U.S. fundraising campaign based in Boston to raise money for Nelson Mandela's election in 1994—I worked with members of the Anti-Apartheid movement all over the U.S. as well as with exiled ANC members.

One volunteer, Rider, was in his late 20s. He was an ANC youth fighter from the townships outside of Johannesburg and was exiled to Zimbabwe. While in Zimbabwe he received a scholarship to study at MIT in Cambridge, MA. One day we were talking about doing a literature drop to build a crowd for a rally we were having, and he suggested we go to the top of the tallest building in Boston, The Prudential Building, put all the leaflets in a metal trash can, and explode it to send the leaflets falling all over the city. Instead we leafleted the student union, went door to door on Massachusetts Avenue, which runs through the MIT campus, and posted signs in the dormitories.

Rider asked me why so many white people wanted to help South African blacks when they weren't interested in helping out the blacks in the U.S.

I love it when people question your motives and help you to reshape the way you look at things. Rider did—and continues to do—this to me, with that one question.

My answer then still seems to hold true for me today: Because it is easier. It is easier to clean other people's closets than to clear out your own. You don't have the lifelong memories attached to each article of clothing, each photo, or each single earring.

But our adventure in the RV can't just be about seeing the scrubbed-up, made-for-public-consumption, gift-shop-and-café version of the U.S. We need to see the truth and not just do the easy thing.

Will New Jack City and the garden sheds be on our list of things we want to see on our travels across the U.S.? How can they not? It is the least we can do—to open our eyes, to hear the stories of the people who live there.

We need to see the reality to underscore and be aware of our good fortune and to see how we can help to be part of the movement to rebuild the U.S. when we finally park the RV.

Confessions of a Pickup Artist

London

30 April 2009

I pick people up. I always have. An old boyfriend used to accuse me of flirting all the time. I do, but I don't discriminate and I don't think of it as flirting. I am curious. I like people. I am a frustrated sociologist.

I am one of those folks who chat you up as you are waiting in line at the grocery store. And I am getting bolder as I get older.

It's hereditary. One of my earliest childhood memories involves being in the line at the Red Owl grocery store in Minneapolis waiting for my mom as she chatted with her friend. Later in the car I asked how long they had been friends. She looked at me and said, "I just met her in line." Quoting Holly Hobbie and the decoupage plaque on our kitchen wall, mom continued, "There is no such thing as a stranger, just an unmet friend."

Holly Hobbie has been following me around ever since.

When we first moved to London I tried to put my chattiness in a box and wrap it up tight with strapping tape. Chatting people up is not what you do in the U.K. The moral code is to wait until you are introduced. It might be years until you meet your neighbors. The morning and afternoon "school runs" are ridiculous. It took a good four months of walking by the same woman and her kids every single day before she would give me the "Acknowledgement of Your Existence" head bob.

So it goes without saying that when you are in the long queue at the post office, nobody is introducing themselves to the person in front of them and you need to keep quiet.

But the other day there was a woman in front of me who was mailing a large parcel to West Africa. My inner Holly Hobbie was chatting away in my brain, saying: "Mali. The African woman in front of me is mailing something to Mali. I have been to Mali. Should I use one of my 17 words of Bambara and say hello? She would be so surprised to have a middle-aged white woman in the Jewish enclave of Golders Green in North West London speak a few words to her in her mother tongue. It is so cool to have stereotypes blown away. Do it Wendy. Do it. But then my cover will be blown. American. Everyone in the entire post office will know I am an American by my nice teeth and broad accent. Then they will blame me for George Bush and the war and British soldiers dying. They are still mad over the Revolution and our independence."

The line moved too fast and the opportunity was lost, but Holly Hobbie had already ripped off all the layers of strapping tape so she was ready to make an appearance the following week at Sainsbury's Superstore.

I hate the Sainsbury's at the 02 centre on Finchley Road. Big. Impersonal. Always moving the inventory around just to frustrate the customers. Finally, I had finished my shopping. I was second in line at Checkout Counter Number 5. What was that? The checkout woman was singing to herself. Quietly singing, but singing nevertheless.

I knew that song: John Denver's "Back Home Again." One of the first albums I ever owned was *John Denver: Songbook*. I even bought the music book with the money I saved up from babysitting so I could play my guitar in my bedroom with the door closed and pretend I was on stage with John wearing my best poncho.

She came to the second verse. She was faltering. She was losing it. She needed me! I stuck my head around the person in front of me and offered up:

There's all the news to tell him, how'd you spend your time . . .

By the time all my groceries were loaded into the shopping bags from the conveyor belt, we had made it through "Annie's Song" and even a pretty good attempt at "Thank God I'm a Country Boy." The other customers were pretending to ignore us but I could see they were moving their lips to the words. I suggested we take over the PA system and serve as the live entertainment at Checkout Counter Number 5.

Maybe we could meet after her shift ended and we could pick up some extra cash busking at the Finchley Road tube station.

Maybe this was the beginning of a new career, or at least a "Sing-a-long at Sainsbury's" night.

As we head out on the road this coming year, one thing that worries me is being lonely. Yes, there is Evan and the boys, but I need a good chat from time to time. But not to fear, I will just channel my inner Holly Hobbie and keep my eyes open for an unmet friend.

The View from My Window

London

15 May 2009

I know I should brush my teeth after every meal, but in reality I brush twice a day, after breakfast and before bed. I have one of those fancy Braun electric toothbrushes—two minutes for the whole process, not including flossing. While I brush I look out the window of my bathroom, which is attached to our bedroom in the loft.

When we bought our ca. 1911 house in London in November of 2006, the third floor was a scary place accessible only by way of a nasty ladder placed through a square hole in the second-floor ceiling. The previous owners, Mr. and Mrs. Harvey, had lived in the house for 50 years, and this was where they kept their old luggage, sleds (a remnant from when snow was more predictable in London), and ancient sports equipment. It was also the home of the open water tank, which was a catalyst for a series of bizarre dreams of open sewers and drowning rats.

Before we moved in, we ripped off the roof and built out the third floor with dormers. A staircase was added, complete with heart-shaped cutouts on the banister. The third floor is where the master bedroom and en suite bathroom is. The views are tremendous. It is our own private tree house looking out over the Memorial Gardens of the Hoop Lane Crematorium.

I start brushing my teeth in the bathroom, looking out the small window by the sink, but my view is obstructed on the left by the gables that go over the storage room. I then walk into the bedroom with toothbrush still in mouth and look out. Directly behind our garden fence are three giant poplar trees. They remind me of France and the long driveways that lead up to the chateaus in the Loire Valley that are flanked on either side by rows of poplars. Last spring all the neighbors abutting the Memorial Gardens were sent notices from the Barnet Council saying there was a petition to cut down the poplars, along with a number of other trees, proposed by the Hoop Lane Crematorium and Memorial Gardens. A neighbor started a letter-writing campaign and the tree cutters were denied. A victory for the trees! The Lorax would be proud.

The previous owner's son told me that both of his parents were cremated there and he and his brother had planted some flowering azaleas in the memorial garden in their memory. I have tried to find the azaleas but so far, without success.

The first fall we lived in London, while Evan was at work and Josh was at school, Simon and I would explore the area in his Maclaren buggy. One of the first places we found was the Memorial Gardens. At a year and a half he would toddle all over the gardens, looking at the pretty flowers, searching for those that smelled best.

From the window you can watch the appearance and disappearance of nearby buildings, depending on the foliage. One of the buildings is St Jude's on the Hill, an Anglican Church in the heart of the Hampstead Garden Suburb. Another building is the Children's Gazebo. This is where parents, families, friends, and relatives go to place flowers, stuffed animals, and notes to children who have died. This view I will not be sorry to say good-bye to. However, it helps me keep things in check. It reminds me to hug my boys a little harder, to keep my life in perspective, and to appreciate the moments we are together because life is so fleeting.

I also look directly down on our own garden. I see the shed we all painted one Sunday in the spring when my brother and sister-in-law and niece used to live across town; the swing set where Josh and Simon and loads of their friends have spent hours swinging, playing, and talking; the beds of flowers and trees I have planted these last couple of years; and the bamboo that is growing nicely in front of the playhouse. When we were designing the garden Simon really wanted to plant bamboo to attract pandas.

From my window I see our neighbor Julie's Bramley apple tree, and it is magnificent. She shares the bounty so I can make pies, and she makes her apple jelly. She has a tire swing attached to a lower branch. At 87 she is rarely on the swing, but it is a fine invitation to her younger friends, whom she often entertains.

In preparation for our move, I asked her if she would be interested in anything from our garden. We decided she should have the teak bench that was Mrs. Harvey's, since the two of them had a 50-year friendship and their sons had grown up together. Julie used to see Mrs. Harvey giving her music lessons to her students sitting on the bench in the garden.

Over the next year the view as I brush my teeth will be changing—sometimes from morning until night. I won't have memories associated with these particular new views, but I wonder what other memories they will trigger during those two minutes twice a day. Maybe I will start brushing after lunch as well.

Sunday Night Book Group

London Tube

Northern Line

Golders Green to Hampstead Station

31 May 2009

It is Sunday night and I am off to book group
Don't get in my way
I need to be there come what may

I am off to book group
I don't care if the kids are sick
I don't care if I've got work to do

I am off to book group . . .

With half the book read
The kitchen is a mess
The laundry is piled high
The phone calls aren't returned

But I don't care
Book group is for me
Book group is my free therapy

I'll drink my glass of wine and chat with my girlfriends about:
kids, husbands, in-laws, work, politics, art shows, theater, movies, old
boyfriends, poetry, weight loss, weight gain, restaurants, schools,
memories, old letters, aging parents, childbirth, menopause, thoughts,
observations, religion, morals, ethics, cultural taboos.

And on occasion . . . the book.

It is Sunday night and I am here at book group
Reading to my friends whom I love and treasure
Like my favorite books.

403 Boxes of Our Lives

Bathroom floor of the Marriott Hotel

Swiss Cottage, London

29 June 2009

Pickford's Moving Company just pulled away from the curb. They were here for four days packing up our lives into 403 boxes. They came back on the fifth day to move all the boxes into a sea-tight metal container that sat on a huge 18-wheeler in front of the house. The container will be transported onto a boat in Dover, England, and sail off to Boston Harbor. From there it will go through customs and then onto another moving truck and reappear at our storage facility in Framingham, Massachusetts in four to six weeks.

Unless the ship sinks. Which doesn't sound too bad to me right now.

As I look over the 14 pages of inventory that catalogs the 403 boxes I am amazed by:

1. How quickly your life can be put in a box—or at least the stuff. The bigger question of course is how many boxes of memories have we collected? Memories are a lot cheaper to move, and they don't strain your back to pack up. I can hear the truck backing down the loading dock now: "Beep beep beep; incoming pallet of memory boxes; remember to lift with your legs, not your back!"

2. I married a Jewish guy and we have seven boxes of Christmas decorations but only one box with menorahs, haggadahs, plastic Seder plates, and finger puppets of the plagues.

3. Josh at 11 years old has 18 boxes of stuff; Simon at 7 years has 6. There must be some sort of algorithm that works out an estimation of accumulation of stuff by year of life.

4. All we need for our life in the RV fits in eight suitcases—and half of that we could live without.

5. How I am fantasizing about the ship carrying our 403 boxes across the Atlantic being abducted by pirates. What is the resale value on the Somalia black market for vats of Legos? Crate and Barrel dining room chairs? 139 stuffed animals?

6. How much money, time, and energy are spent on the transference of stuff—moving it all from store to home to shelf to box to container to storage facility to new home.

7. All of the pioneers, immigrants, and refugees who have moved by either choice, fear, force, love, or war. How lucky am I to be moving by choice, with options.

Behind the Wheel

But what I can't put in a box are my friends. The walks on Hampstead Heath that seem so natural. The smell of the roses. The green grocer on the high street who sells the bags of tomatoes for 1 pound each. The sneaky walkways that make getting around this city so delightful and old worldly.

More for the memory box in my mind where there is always room and there is no charge for additional weight.

SECTION II — Back in the U.S.A

Notes upon Re-entry

In-laws' house

Long Island, New York

June 24, 2009

We are back in the U.S.A! Did anyone miss us? Did anybody notice we were gone? Six years is a long time. To quote Simon, "Six years is forever when you are seven."

We dropped Josh at a four-week YMCA summer camp in Western Massachusetts with our fingers crossed he would have the time of his life. Then Evan, Simon, and I drove to Roswell, GA, to clear out our storage facility, which was full of crap we hadn't seen for six years. Funny how when someone else was paying the storage facility bill we kept a lot of unnecessary stuff. We loaded up the car 10 times, bringing load after load to the Goodwill.

While we were in Roswell, I spent some time thinking about what's hitting me upon being back to the U.S. I don't mean any of this in a judgmental way, just observational:

- File this one under Profound Observations of the Absurdly Obvious but lots of people have American accents here in the U.S.A. I am not unique or exotic anymore.

- Checks. Places still accept checks for payment. It seems so provincial—a harkening back to a time of trust. I am having trouble remembering how to fill in a check.

- Did I get skinny or did Americans get really fat? The ploy I introduced back in 1987 to offer cookies and candy bars to everyone to help them get fat so I would look smaller in comparison really took off while we were gone. Little did I realize McDonald's had the same strategy . . . and Burger King, and KFC, and Chick-fil-A. I feel positively svelte. Think I will have another piece of chocolate cake.

- Drivers in this country are tough. The MO seems to be "Don't use your turn signals—you don't want to give the enemy information." In the U.K. when drivers turn on their signal, the people in the next lane slow down and . . . let them in! In the U.S., once you turn on your clicker it is a challenge for your fellow racers on the interstate—drive faster and close the gap between cars.

- Miss Wendy. They call me Miss Wendy in the American South.

- Can we talk restrooms—public restrooms? Clean! Even the one at the park, the gas station, Jones Beach on Long Island. I am back in the land of two-ply toilet paper. To paraphrase Lee Greenwood,"I am proud to be an American where the public restrooms are clean."

- God is everywhere. Complete strangers are ready, willing, and able—not to mention excited—to talk about their personal experience with the Lord Jesus Christ.

One afternoon, I was waiting to get the car repaired in Atlanta off Peachtree Industrial. Something was up with the transmission. The television in the waiting room was turned on to the 700 Club and the man on the screen was giving testimony to how the horrible facial rash that had plagued him for the past three years had mysteriously disappeared through the miracle of prayer. Here I was expecting him to start pitching the organic facial cream that could be yours for$19.99 but no—it was nothing less than divine intervention.

I watched this for about a minute and was shaking my head in disbelief. So many differences between the U.K. and U.S. from a clean waiting room in an auto repair store to a working television broadcasting a God program. Is this legal?

I was snickering to myself, thinking of how different this experience was to CB Motors in the U.K., where I used to bring our old stick shift Volvo. There was no waiting room at CB Motors, let alone a TV, and given the small grimy office I never dreamed of asking about a restroom.

My thoughts were interrupted by a gentleman sitting on a cushioned chair two seats over in the waiting area. He said, in a very polite voice, "Ma'am, may I ask you a question?"

"Sure," I said, thinking he might want to change the channel.

"Ma'am, I noticed you were smilin' at the television and I just want to know if you believe?"

"Believe in what?" I blurted out naively. I thought, "No! This guy can't really be asking me if I believe in God is a car repair waiting area!"

I was mistaken. It wasn't my belief in God he was interested in. He asked, "Do you believe in the Lord God Jesus Christ?"

"It is complicated . . . " I started to reply, thinking he might actually be interested in having a conversation about the bigger picture of God and how wonderful it was that he, my fellow patron here at the auto repair on Peachtree Industrial, had found something to believe in. But no, he didn't want a discussion. He wanted an audience.

It takes a lot to shut me down. I was shut down.

Praise the Lord and let there be some divine intervention on my transmission here at the car repair on Peachtree Industrial to get me out of this conversation!

Welcome back to the U.S. of A.

Downwardly Mobile Home Ownership

In-laws' house

Long Island, New York

June 26, 2009

On our drive back up from Georgia, on I-95 outside of Washington D.C., we bought an RV. Oh brother. This is really happening.

It is a Winnebago Itasca Impulse. It is new. It is clean. It has cream interior with a sporty strip. It has a microwave and a slide-out. A slide-out is very tricky invention. It is a sneaky button you push—once you are stopped and the parking brake is set—that literally slides out the living room section of the RV and makes it about a third wider. Wide enough to dance? Just.

It isn't nearly as horrible as I thought it would be. And I mean that in a good way. Evan and I have a private bedroom in the back with a queen-size bed. There are shelves above the bed and even a little closet to hang things up. I hadn't thought about bringing clothes that would necessitate a hanger on the trip. That opens up whole new possibilities. Skirts. Dresses. An iron. Do I want to iron on the RV trip?

The boys have a queen-size bed up above the cab. There is room on the sides for them to put their few stuffed animals and assorted knickknacks.

There is a nice-size refrigerator and freezer, a bathroom with a toilet and sink, and a shower stall on the other side of the tiny hallway.

We can store food under the seats of the dinette.

All of our needs will be met.

But there is no place to store an ironing board. Well, that takes care of that question.

Jetlag, Kids, and the Birth of Family Traditions

In-laws' house

Long Island, New York

June 30, 2009

I am an early riser. I love that sneaky time before anyone else is up and you can imagine what life must have been like before cars. I love the freshness of the air and the promise of possibilities. The Hindus believe the early morning is the most sacred because it is when God is closest to earth.

When our kids were born I stopped liking the early morning so much because it wasn't my choice anymore. After I had been up half the night, 5:00 A.M. was not my sneaky alone time anymore—it was the fourth shift.

And then we moved to London and each summer we would make the long journey back to my in-laws' house (GMT-5) or my mom's house (GMT-8) and all of a sudden 4:00 A.M. felt like midday.

What do you do when you are wide awake at 4:00 A.M. with a four-year-old and an eight-year-old in a house of sleeping elderly parents?

This, my friend, is where The Pajama Adventure was born.

Our mornings went like this:

4:00–5:00 A.M. Cuddle in bed and have sneaky chats in the dark about what we want to do that day and how excited we are to be with Grandma and Grandpa. Only rule: stay in bed.

5:00–6:00 A.M. Small light on, quiet book reading. Sometimes a nap.

6:00 A.M. Enough already. We have bedsores, we are BORED, and we are going nuts being quiet. Out the door. In pajamas.

If the truth be told, I never had enough foresight to lay out clothes the night before, and making the noise to rumble through bags at 6:00 A.M. wasn't an option. But then the boys and I decided life is a whole lot more exciting if you are doing something a bit unexpected—a little naughty— and wearing your pajamas outside fits the bill.

Places we have been at 6:00 A.M. in pajamas:

- Playgrounds. No competition for the good swings.

- Beaches. Have you ever watched the steam rise from a Vermont pond at sunrise?

- Other people's gardens. There is a lot of wild lawn art out there. Counting cement frogs and searching for garden gnomes kills quite a bit of time.

- Swimming pools. Hotel pools usually open at 6:00 A.M.

- Grounds of historical landmarks. Yes, that was us in pajamas on Abraham Lincoln's front lawn in Springfield, IL, at 6:17 A.M. Adventure Walks. Stick the word *adventure* in front of anything and it becomes a whole lot more interesting. These Adventure Walks usually covered one block only, but who knew what we would find!

- Donut shops. Pajama Adventures always end at the local donut shop. Who else is open that early?

Given there is only a three-hour time difference from the east coast to the west coast, and since we will be going slowly in the RV, I don't think jetlag will be an issue for awhile.

"RV Lag"—hmm, not the same ring.

Transparencies
Bondville, Vermont

July 28, 2009

We are moved into our rental house in Bondville, Vermont for the next three weeks. It is the same lovely big house we have rented for the past five years and it feels like home. Given the upheaval in our lives it is wonderful to be someplace familiar as we organize the RV and get everything ready to head out next month.

I am starting to see this trip in front of us as a map of the U.S. with various passion transparencies laid on top.

Simon's passions: Volcanoes, tropical fish, and panda bears.

Josh's passion: Polar bears.

Evan's passions: Music, technology, baseball parks.

As I was explaining this to a friend the other day, she asked me where my passion transparency was. At the time I told her mine was more of an inward journey—to take an hour to write each day, to take an hour to exercise each day, to play my guitar and prepare a set to play out as a busker when we finally land.

On second thought, this entire journey is my passion. To have my husband and kids all together for an entire year before the kids run away and start their own lives.

To connect the dots of the friends and family for my children.

My transparency is the one where friends and family live. We are connecting the dots in the RV. This trip is about helping us to reconnect with people in our lives and seeing how they live. The passion of a frustrated anthropologist/sociologist. I am a busybody wanting to get into the heads of others and muck about. I like to look for ideas, inspiration, and new ways of seeing things from my friends and steal what I like in an effort to help me make sense of the world.

Back in 1992 I took six months and traveled around the world, staying with friends and family who were conveniently located everywhere from Mali to Germany, Uganda, India, Singapore, and Australia. I realized midway through that trip that I was observing couples and how they interacted, as well as single people and their relationships with their communities and how they worked and lived with the cultural differences. While this trip isn't as exotic culturally, I think it will have depth in terms of observation and thoughtfulness.

My passion is to teach my children the importance of connections.

Their connections to people—be they related or not.
Their connections to the U.S.
Their connections to the land.
Their connections to each other and Evan and me.
Their connections to situations, including how they can be agents of change.

We are all stronger and wiser for having made connections with others—however they work out.

Thanks, Lisa, for asking the question and making me think.

Major League Freak-out

Bondville, Vermont

July 30, 2009

What are we doing? We can't possibly leave in two weeks.

We have yet to open up a big map of the U.S.A. We have a GPS but we need a huge map of the U.S. to lay out on the floor and get acquainted with. Yesterday Josh asked where Cincinnati was. He thought it was in the American South. How can we possibly be ready to go if Josh doesn't know where Cincinnati is?

We need to touch the map. Walk around it. Put pins in it. Plan more than we have. Hell, we haven't planned at all . . . well, maybe a little.

We have not completed the curriculum for the kids' schooling. Let alone register properly with the State of Vermont so THEY (the government?) can put our boys on their records as homeschoolers.

We have to get ourselves registered as Vermont residents and voters, and get our driver licenses.

Neither the car nor the RV is registered. Where are we going to park the car for the year?

Evan and I still don't have doctors.

The container arrives from London on Tuesday in Framingham, MA.

I think I might drive the Big Pig to Framingham to get used to it. I want to drive it by myself so no one will hear me swear.

Plus there are 10 boxes of stuff for the RV we packed up in London in the container that we will need to transport. What is in those boxes? Winter clothes. Kitchen stuff. Bedding. Bicycles.

We need to completely outfit the Big Pig. Organize our stuff and make sure it all fits.

We need to make the beds.

Silverware. We don't have any silverware.

I don't know what half of the buttons are for in the Big Pig.

A name. We need a name for the Big Pig. While I kind of like Big Pig, it has a sort of negative feel. The RV needs a proper name. A friend recommended Petunia. I like it, but again it has a certain porcine quality. Then there is Wilbur of *Charlotte's Web* fame. But with Swine Flu, perhaps not sensitive to the times.

Is the RV a male or a female? How can we live in an RV if we don't even know if it is a boy or a girl? Simon said the RV talked to him and his name is Chuck.

Simon said only people under the age of 20 can hear the RV talk.

My son talks to RVs.

Is this RV trip supposed to be fun? Is this the scared part of the "excited and scared" combination that I used to say I was always looking for? But that was before I had kids and aging parents. I feel very irresponsible.

Am I having a conversation with myself as I write? Am I nuts? How can an insane person be given the responsibility to drive an RV? Maybe I need to talk to Simon and see how the RV feels about having me drive it.

We can't leave in two weeks. Who are we kidding?

But maybe in three weeks.

Whew. That makes me feel better.

Four New Things All in One Day

Bondville, Vermont

August 7, 2009

At 46 years old sometimes I am reluctant to try new things.

Quite frankly, at 46 years old there are not that many new things that present themselves in the course of a day to try.

At 46 years old I know the consequences of trying new things and, while I hate to admit it, I know that my body doesn't bounce back as quickly in case the new thing I try doesn't turn out as expected.

An incident involving a push scooter, a bottle of wine, an unexpected pothole, and a heroic save on my part of a certain son on a promenade in Paris still haunts my right knee on wet days.

But then there was Thursday.

We were at Bromley Mountain in Southern Vermont. In the winter it is a lovely place to go skiing. In the summer for the past 30 years they have offered rides on an alpine slide. First you take the chairlift up the mountain, and then you throw yourself into a small cart on wheels to plummet your way down the mountain in a graphite chute to the tune of 30 miles per hour. But I have done the alpine slide for years—nothing new there.

However, over the past 10 years or so, they have continued to add new, better, faster, more exciting things to do to entice the ADD crowd.

So here is what I did:

Space bike. I strapped myself in, with my trusty husband at my side, to a bicycle and got whipped around upside down on a circular track. Ride time: about 3 minutes. Recovery time: about 2 hours.

Rock wall. Sure I have seen these all over town. My kids have been to birthday parties where this was the main activity. But for me? The harness alone is enough to turn me off. And the answer is, yes, your butt looks enormous in the rock climbing gear. But one of the benefits of 46 is that I don't care anymore. I climbed the wall! There were four options ranging in difficulty. I started at 1. Mastered on the first go. I continued up 2. Check. I thought about 3, but no! Saved by the bell. It was time to head up to the third NEW THING of the day.

Sun Mountain Flyer. As their website explains:

"It cost $1,000,000 to build. It soars as high as a five-story building. It approaches speeds of 50 MPH. At one-half-mile long, it's the longest thrill ride of its kind in New England, one of only three on the east coast, and one of only ten in the world. It's the Sun Mountain Flyer, the Sun

Mountain Adventure Park's new double-line ZipRider®, and it's like no ride you've experienced, anywhere. Prepare to meet thy zoom!"

What this means is that you take the chairlift up. Climb a fire tower. Strap yourself into a diaper/chair thing with lots of hooks with the help of a mostly together, however slightly disinterested, 18-year-old with assorted tattoos. And then they push you out the flap of a door so you can zip down the mountain, building up speeds to 50 miles an hour. It is fast, it is beautiful overlooking the Vermont valley, and it is not too scary. I felt like I was flying . . . until the end when the swing caught on a stopper and I got whipped up and flung back and poured out onto a platform. Ride Time: about 30 seconds. Recovery time: 1 hour.

And then . . . and then . . .

The Red Fox Inn. This old roadhouse has been a steady friend over the past 15 years or so. It is a beautiful 1.2 mile walk from our rental house, and in the summer it's very casual. The bar serves food and kids are welcome and on Thursdays it is Open Mic Night.

We sat up next to the stage and chatted with Mike, the guitarist for the house band. The drummer, Adam, let the kids have a go on his drum kit. My husband, friend Mary from London, and her two kids, along with mine, encouraged me, rallied me. I couldn't ignore the growing drumbeat any longer. Mike gladly relinquished his guitar. Adam gave me a backup beat and I PLAYED "PUFF THE MAGIC DRAGON" ON THE STAGE AT THE RED FOX INN!

And the best part was that Simon did his interpretive dance while I played. Playing time: 5 minutes tops. Recovery time: 3 days and counting.

Phew. What a day.

Major League Freak-out #2
Bondville, Vermont

August 15, 2009

We are well on our way to solving a lot of the issues. Alright, Evan has solved a lot of the issues.

Our kids are registered as homeschoolers for the State of Vermont. I have the official piece of paper! Why does an official piece of paper make me feel so much better? Validation!

We both have VT driver licenses. Again, another piece of validation.

The RV is registered in VT.

We have a Vermont address so now we can register to vote. We are official residents.

I made the bed in the RV in the Target parking lot in Milbury, Massachusetts and then took a nap . . . in the RV. In the Target parking lot. Strangely surreal and peaceful.

We have doctor appointments scheduled for Monday.

I have driven the Big Pig for over 200 miles and I haven't hit anything. I ran over a few curbs but that is to be expected. I even backed it down a long driveway. Note to future self: Look into changing careers to truck driver.

I have turned on the generator.

All of our guests are gone and we have four days to pack up and move out on to the road.

First stop: Baseball Hall of Fame.

Heading Out Letter

Bondville, Vermont

August 15, 2009

Dear Friends and Family,

It is Saturday afternoon the 15th of August. I am writing you from the Green Mountains of Vermont, where we are now official residents, wear tie-dye every day, and flash the peace sign as we drive past folks on the dirt roads. Evan and the boys are making blueberry jam from the buckets of blueberries we picked yesterday, and we are listening to an interesting combination of Green Day, Weird Al, and "The Simpsons Sing the Blues." I am sorting through lists, freaking out, and eating chocolate.

We have had an action-packed summer cleaning out our storage facility in Roswell, Georgia, road tripping up the East Coast, and playing in Vermont at the holiday house with a ton of fabulous friends who have helped us keep our sanity while we took care of the details for our Adventure Year! We are registered to vote, we have new driver licenses, and the homeschooling curriculum we put together is all approved by the VT Dept of Education. All our stuff (over 500 boxes from both the U.K. and Georgia) is in a storage facility in Framingham, Massachusetts. Don't get me started on the stuff conversation.

We are getting into the RV this Wednesday the 19th of August—four days behind schedule. But wait a minute! Whose schedule are we on? We just revised the schedule. Never mind.

Our new home is a 29-foot Winnebago Itasca Impulse. We will be holding a Name the RV Contest on our website with the winner receiving a jar of the previously mentioned homemade jam! Right now I keep calling it the Big Pig. Simon calls it Chuck. It clearly needs some help!

If you haven't checked out our website and all our blogs lately—do so! (www.familyadventureyear.com) At this point, the website also has a calendar that is reasonably up-to-date with our itinerary through the end of 2009. We plan to update the 2010 itinerary in October. Evan still has not finished the integration with Flickr (for photo sharing) or the button that lets you see where we've been on a map. The website also shows where we are at any given point in time (Evan can update it from his BlackBerry, but we're not planning to update it more than once a day).

Our hope is to send out monthly updates to our Google Group email list (you can sign up on the left-hand side of our website). If you know someone else who wants to sign up, go to the left side of our website and enter the email address and then click the "Subscribe" button. If you're

Behind the Wheel

having trouble, send Evan an email at evan@familyadventureyear.com and he'll sign you up for it.

Here are some blog highlights:

Homeless No More and RSVP: Evan's blog about the American South and the RV, with photos!

Notes Upon Reentry and 4 New Things: Wendy's Blog about coming back to the U.S. with too many self-absorptions.

Bromley Mountain and Turkeys: Simon's blogs about life as a seven-year-old.

Penguins, Summer Camp, and Poet William Cowper: Josh's blogs about life as a 12-year-old.

Peace, love, admiration, adoration, and clean laundry to you all!

Wendy, Evan, Josh, and Simon

36 Hours Until Departure
Bondville, Vermont

August 17, 2009

Simon is so sad. He misses London so much. "Mommy, London is the only home I know. I miss our house. I am excited about the big adventure, but right now I am so sad."

Me too. I know this is the right thing to do and it really is the chance of a lifetime, but mostly I am tired of moving and we haven't even begun.

Simon took an empty cardboard box and excitedly suggested we could make a replica of our old house from it. "That way we can take it with us all the time." Josh suggested we have a special Anniversary Day for the house so we can all tell each other things we remember.

We will do both suggestions. And look at pictures. And write letters to our friends. But it still makes us sad.

I have always maintained that the kids would take their cues from Evan and me and that if we put on a brave face and make whatever trouble or trying time we are going through into an adventure, then they would rise up and all would be well.

But my brave faced melted as I was lying in Simon's bed and we were crying together into his pillow.

But he is asleep now and tomorrow is another day.

We need to make the RV more of a home . . . starting tomorrow. I can't call it the Big Pig anymore and expect my kids will feel like it is a nice place to call home. While it isn't really a "home" it will be the one thing that will remain constant in our lives over the upcoming months.

Time to paint the walls, put up the artwork, organize our blankets and stuffed animals, and start thinking of the RV as our respite rather than a joke.

I guess this really is our life . . . for now.

12 Hours and Counting . . . Not that I Am Counting
Bondville, Vermont

August 18, 2009

Is this the calm before the storm? Will there be a storm? There just was a storm—with a ton of thunder thrown in—an hour ago. Tomorrow night in the RV park. Oh god, another anxiety nightmare—we could be in a tin box in a lightning storm. Cue the visual of the lightning bolt hitting the RV Toaster. Four pieces of bread that look suspiciously like Evan, the boys, and me are popping out slots at the top and we all have permed hair . . .

Simon was better today. During the day he decided to ditch the idea of making a cardboard box into a replica of our old house in London because he was feeling better. He drew a bundle of pictures to put up in the RV, even a picture of a Dream Eater that eats the bad dreams and puffs out beautiful dreams. I think I might need that picture above my head tonight to keep away the thoughts of lightning frying the RV.

But then this evening before dinner I found him in our bed, quietly sobbing, saying he just couldn't go on the trip at all. Evan overheard us chatting about his worries and suggested that after a dinner of pizza we could spend some time in the RV looking at all the cool storage boxes (always a crowd pleaser!) and then have a Family Meeting to discuss Simon's feelings and to have a general check-in about the trip.

Simon perked right up. I'm not sure if it was the pizza, the storage boxes, or the chance to be highlighted on the Family Meeting agenda. We have been holding Family Meetings pretty regularly for the past five years, and Simon is very familiar with the format. To have your item first—with your name right next to the topic—makes you feel that you are special and that you are being heard. Isn't that what we all want? To be heard? To be first on the agenda? Having our needs addressed?

Family Meeting Agenda

    I.   Simon's worries

   II.   Pace of the next couple of weeks

  III.   What we need to do before we leave tomorrow

  IV.   Thanksgiving plans (Evan's parents were over and we wanted to be sure we talked about when we would see them next)

For Item I, Simon's worries, we all discussed how overwhelming the thought of the trip is and how thinking about living in an RV for such a long time makes us want to scream. Starting anything new can be scary and can make you want to scream. Simon and I went out on the balcony and screamed a really good long scream and felt better.

Talk calmly. Go outside and scream. Come back in and continue the conversation. This is normal, yes?

We then came inside and we all discussed how we were excited about the first couple of weeks.

Tomorrow we head out to Cooperstown to the Baseball Hall of Fame. Simon got all excited about seeing Babe Ruth's bat, and Grandpa told us some stories about The Babe and Lou Gehrig.

We decided that we would leave tomorrow as planned but we will check in once we are in St. Louis next week to see how we are feeling. But then we remembered that my mom, Mama Jo, is coming to meet us in Springfield, and then there is the family reunion and we get to stay at Aunt Jackie and Uncle Paul's house and they have a sneaky clubhouse with a trap door and everything. So, we decided to just think about the trip up until then.

Phew. I like this idea too. A whole school year in an RV is too long to think about.

What is that old line? How do you eat an elephant? One bite at a time. I have to say, I prefer a year in an RV to eating an elephant . . .

Section III — On the Road

Day 1 - So Far So Good?
RV Park — Springfield, New York

August 19, 2009

It is 9:50 P.M. We made it a little more than 150 miles today to East Springfield, NY. Just a quick drive from Cooperstown so we will be ready for the Baseball Hall of Fame tomorrow. Why a family who has no hand/eye coordination is interested in baseball I don't know.

We are parked in a level spot. We plugged in our new home on wheels to the water and electricity here at the RV park. We went for a swim, had dinner, took a walk, and now bed.

What a ridiculous day. I was up at 6:00 A.M. wallowing in the details to get out of the rental house. Loading up the RV. Bringing suitcases, boxes, a suitcase filled with suitcases, and books to Evan's parents' place in Vermont to store. Yes, all this is in addition to the 534 boxes in the official storage facility. Does that number keep getting larger and larger the more I tell it? "Did you hear about Wendy and all her boxes in storage? I heard she was up to 4,328 boxes! And more than half are filled with useless plastic objects!"

My version of hell: A house filled with miniature toy poodles and Chihuahuas, lima beans, and useless plastic objects.

And then . . . the 8-hour rant by an unnamed older son telling Evan and me what useless parents we are as we drove those 150 miles. How we just don't understand and that we are violating his rights and have no respect for him.

Why? Because we aren't going to drive six hours out of our way to see his good friend. Just because we are in New York and so is his friend doesn't mean said friend is close by. New York is a big state.

I don't know if I can handle living in an RV being told continually that I am an uncompassionate human being. We were thinking this would be a sans alcohol RV. I am beginning to reconsider that policy on the first day.

But it really is all quite cozy. Our little bedroom is comfortable. Everything works. Oh no, delete that line, don't want to jinx anything. If all goes well I will get up at 6:00 A.M. and take that hour-long bike ride through the beautiful New York State countryside. Yes, I will ride back to the RV. I think.

Day 3 - And Then

Hwy 90 — Somewhere in New York State

August 22, 2009

Some of the things I love about my firstborn are his creativity and willingness to learn. Yes, he has a sense of justice that just won't quit, and while it is incredibly tiring to be on the other side of the head butting, I admire his persistence. As Evan likes to say about his sales prospects: "It isn't so much about winning them over as it is about wearing them down."

So this is what we did in terms of meeting up with his friend: We kind of submitted. Josh did some research and came up with a proposal that would include driving for two hours, boondocking (sleeping in a Walmart parking lot for free), and making an acceptable drive on the following day. I pitched it to the other family, but they couldn't do it. Hooray! A double win for the parents! Josh learned the importance of research and advanced planning and we kept on track . . . not that there is that much of a track to keep to.

What turned me around from my position of "not driving out of our way a single iota" to splitting the difference was that on Wednesday night he and his friend had an hour-long phone conversation. Afterward, Josh and I had a chat. Another thing I love about Josh is that he still likes to chat. I am trying to instill in my boys that chatting is good and so they should keep doing it. Cool guys chat. Chatty boys get the girls. Chatty boys have more fun.

Josh mentioned how hard it is for guys to stay in touch. He is worried that he will drift away from his friends. So am I. Friends and family are key to a person's happiness. That sense of belonging to a community is priceless. Josh is getting older. He is putting together a community of his own that I need to respect and encourage. Get over yourself Wendy; it isn't about your schedule. And another brilliant point made by My Personal Help Desk (aka Evan) was that this trip is also about showing the kids that we can be flexible and spontaneous.

I am trying to keep up my hour a day of exercise and an hour of writing. Today I took a beautiful bike ride along County Road 31 in East Springfield, NY. Lots of farms. I biked to a state park—Glimmerglass. It was 7:30 when I biked in. Nobody was around. Who would have thought that the oldest covered bridge in the U.S. would be there? 1867. That used to sound old to me, but now that I am an International Snob that sounds like recent history. Give me something from the roman age—now that is old.

Behind the Wheel

We live in an RV. I still don't believe it. We drive with all our stuff with us, all the time. Simon and I danced in the Big Pig this morning. There was room to do a couple of spins.

We had lunch today in a rest area off the highway. Pizza bagels. Noodles. We have a budget of 110 bucks a day. Goes fast when you have a 45 gallon tank to fill at $3 a gallon. I look at money very differently now that there is nothing coming in. Invite us to dinner and we might steal stuff out of your pantry—this is your warning.

I am now typing away as we are barreling down the New York Turnpike on our way to Buffalo, and then up we go into Canada to see Niagara Falls.

Bruce Springsteen is singing "Keep your eye on the prize, roll on" from his *Live in Dublin* album, the boys are plugged into an iTouch watching *The Simpsons Movie*. Don't worry, Evan is driving.

From Niagara to an Oasis to Another Springfield

On the road in Ohio . . . or maybe Indiana . . .

August 25, 2009

The first three nights on the road were a bit of a learning experience. Here is what we do when we get into camp:

Back up our 29-foot, 15,000-pound home into the proper level spot.
Set the emergency brake.
Make sure the area is clear for the slide-out.
Plug in the shore line to juice up the electric.
Attach the water connection.
Pull out the awning/porch cover.
Unlock and pull off the bicycles.
Put the tablecloth on the picnic table.
Find some flowers for the table and set with the fine china . . . or plastic plates from Tesco.

After Cooperstown we went up to Niagara Falls. Hmmm. After all was said and done, this committee says: Yes! Keep Niagara on the list of places to go. Just don't stay at Jellystone RV Park . . . way too depressing.

Why I thought I should trust Yogi Bear—an animated character known for stealing picnic baskets in the 1960s—over a state park is beyond me. It is a parking lot of RVs—and huge RVs that make our 29-footer look like a MINI Cooper next to a Hummer. I think I saw a tree—or maybe it was a cell tower pretending to be a tree.

And if you want to go to Niagara, start saving your money now because Niagara Falls is a Disneyland Attraction. But some things you just have to do. I mean, *Maid of the Mist*. Say no more. Once you see the falls you want to go near them, in them, under them, and the boat ride is the closest you can do it without risking your life. Why people want to keep throwing themselves down the falls in boats and barrels I don't understand—*The Maid* was enough for me. They do throw in plastic recyclable rain coats with your $14.95 ticket price—which we are now saving to make a reappearance for Halloween.

But then there was *Niagara's Fury*. So get this . . . we had just been on *Maid of the Mist*. We had just walked along the edge and then rode a boat through the real Niagara Falls. So why did we then need to pay an additional 14 bucks per person to go inside and watch a "4D movie" about what was outside and we had just been in? Humans. I just don't get us.

Side note: We were in Niagara, Ontario, Canada. We had read that the views were better and the schlock not as great. Let me tell you, schlock is alive and well in Ontario. Good news: Our kids never asked for anything in the gift shops. This budget thing is working. They know how much we have to spend a day and putting Josh in charge of keeping us to the daily budget was brilliant! Bad news: I have to keep to it as well. No pedicures for me, and it looks like I am going natural on the hair color as well. Those pretend natural highlights are no longer pretend, nor particularly highlightable either.

And then we drove to our friend's house outside Pittsburgh. Wow. An oasis of calm and beauty. I have known Patty for the past four years and she and her husband and four kids moved back to the U.S. about eight months ago. It was great to spend time with friends who have been through the same issues around re-entry to the U.S.—coming to grips with the fact we aren't Faux Europeans anymore and all the rest. Plus, they are fun and welcoming and gracious and engaging and have a beautiful guest room, a bountiful organic garden, a washer and dryer. And they SHARE! Our kids basically ran out of the RV and disappeared for the next 36 hours.

Patty and I talked about writing. And the importance of when you are a writer, you need to write. Goal: 1,000 words a day. This is word 654.

And now we are in Ohio. We were hoping for Indiana but got sucked into
Target, the grocery store, and then sidelined by an hour of roadworks
outside of Wheeling, West Virginia. Ohio looks good. Hoping all four of us
will do a bike ride down along the lake today. The weather is holding.
Kids are still happy doing chores. Looking forward to fresh tomatoes from
Patty and Harris's garden for lunch.

Tomorrow: St. Louis.

Campground Etiquette

Buck Creek State Park — Springfield, Ohio

August 27, 2009

Dear Gentle Readers,

I am here to tell you there is a certain unspoken etiquette that permeates campground life. For example, here I am at Buck Creek State Park in Springfield, Ohio (yes, another Springfield) and I rolled out of bed in the RV, threw a fleece on over my pajamas and my sandals, and walked to the camp restroom.

I shouldn't have.

Maybe the early morning sunlight that is slowly making its way up over the trees also shined through my nightgown and made it see-through. I don't know, but I got some strange looks from the folks I ran into.

Got that? No wearing your nightgown to the public restroom at 7:23 A.M.

Yours sincerely,

An M. Bare Asssed Camper

FAQs

St. Louis, MO

August 29, 2009

In the seven months of planning . . . and not planning, and procrastinating, and assembling, and researching, and talking with friends, neighbors, relatives, friends and neighbors of relatives, and people we have met in the grocery store checkout line . . . the three questions that people have posed to me (note: not to Evan) the most are:

1. How many pairs of shoes will you bring in the RV?
2. How are you going to keep from going nuts in the RV?
3. How will you have sex in the RV?

I shall address these questions in order of importance.

1. How many pairs of shoes will you bring in the RV?

While I have never thought of myself as a materialistic fashion hound, I have a weakness for shoes. Not that I spend much money on each pair; I am more of a variety and style gal rather than a name brand type.

I blame it on Southwest Junior High School in Minneapolis. 1974. Seventh grade. Adidas. I had to have a pair. Anybody who was anybody wore Adidas. If you had money to burn, you had the green-striped version. Middle of the road, you went for the blue. Strapped for cash meant you had the red. The red ones were $26.00 at the Footlocker at Southdale Shopping Mall in Edina.

I made 50 cents an hour babysitting. I needed the last 5 bucks to get me over the top so I could buy that red pair of entry-level Adidas. New Year's Eve was coming up, excellent babysitting potential.

December 31st found me on the couch of the Andersons watching over their three kids, all under the age of five. I was 12 years old. I was responsible. My mother was a nurse and she would be home and we lived down the street. I was their gal and they needed me from 6:00 P.M. until 3:00 A.M. Score. Got the kids to bed by 7:30, and I settled in with a bowl of ice cream in front of the TV to watch *Invasion of the Body Snatchers* with the fabulous feeling that I would go home with enough money to put me over the edge so I could afford my red Adidas.

Who cared if it snowed 2 feet the day before school started up again in January. I wore my Adidas through the snowdrifts in the bitter cold knowing that my position in the pecking order would be established through my shoes.

Behind the Wheel

Last night I dreamed about my box of shoes in the storage facility. My Moroccan slip-ons; my black lace-up, low-heeled boots from Rome; the 9 West purple pumps with the fake jewels.

So, here is what made it into the black milk crate under the couch in the RV where we all store our shoes. 1. black sandals; 2. brown flip-flops; 3. rubber-soled waterproof Keens and 4. blue running/hiking shoes. And if the CFO approves the requisition order I hope to add a pair of brown boots once it gets colder.

2. How are you going to keep from going nuts in the RV?

The party line: It helps that we all like our own time alone reading, writing, hiking. While yes, this is an intense amount of family time, we also are trying to respect each other's time as individuals.

The truth: We drive each other nuts. Simon is the only one who is consistently in fine form. Josh the pre-adolescent and me the menopausal are at odds every other day, which results in screaming matches that rattle the windows of the RV. Evan and I are alpha control types and in our life prior to the RV he had his fiefdom and I had mine. We respect each other's strengths and try to complement each other where we can. After almost 14 years of marriage and 16 years together this has worked relatively well.

And then there was yesterday . . .

We are staying at my cousin's house for a few nights in the Dogtown section of St. Louis just south of Forest Park. Fabulous location. We can walk to the zoo and the free museums in the park. All is well. The RV is parked out front. We are hoping not to drive it for a few days—stupid to drive it around the city. Evan and I leave the boys in charge of each other while we ride our bicycles to Schnucks Grocery Store. Adorable. We are like college-age coeds with our backpacks on and we head out on this 95-degree day in 97-percent humidity. It is less than a mile. I know the way to go. Evan Google Maps it and finds a better way to go on secondary roads. Fine, until we meet up with the construction project and discover that the road is closed. Back to original way. Nope, Evan needs to make his own, new way. I know where I am. I know where we need to go. But he has his BlackBerry with the map. I have my eyes and my sense of direction!

We both got there and we both got home. Albeit we got home our separate but equal ways. We both have trouble following. But we both trust and respect each other enough and have faith in each other's abilities to get to the same place—sometimes by different routes.

3. How will you have sex in the RV?

Nope. Enough said. Can't go there. And please no more jokes about the bumper sticker: *If it's rockin, don't bother knockin'.*

We Interrupt This RV Trip

Saint Louis, Missouri

August 30, 2009

We interrupt this RV trip to bring you a slice of reality. Mom is moving from San Diego to Phoenix and needs help packing up and moving out. Evan is in charge of the RV and the boys in St. Louis and off I fly on Delta from Saint Louis to Phoenix. The RV is parked in front of my cousin's house and Evan has a cousin in St. Louis as well, so I don't feel as if I am abandoning them (well, maybe a little).

This is one of the reasons we moved back to the U.S.: so we can integrate ourselves back into our extended families' lives, offer help and support, and be there for them if they need us. And now that I have these incredible skills of packing boxes, I really want to use them as much as possible.

I have to say it is weird leaving the RV trip for five nights. Does this mean I am abandoning ship? I am quite conflicted. It is a great feeling to be back in the U.S. and finally be close enough to be helpful to my mom. And Evan is there so I don't need to arrange babysitters and the like.

But still . . . five nights away . . . do I get a per diem so I can eat? Do I have to submit my receipt for the cup of coffee I will pick up at the airport to our 12-year-old RV CFO? Do I get reimbursed? By my son? With my own money?

Which reminds me of an esoteric conversation Josh and I got into regarding Simon and his wiggly tooth and the inevitable Tooth Fairy. How do we budget for the Tooth Fairy? A separate line item called "Magic"? Or is it a line item under "Dental"?

After my brother Garret and I move mom out, she is flying back with me to St. Louis, where the boys and Evan will pick us up so we can drive the 1.5 hours to another Springfield. Springfield, Illinois!

More Questions

35,000 above sea level

August 31, 2009

Wherever I have lived, there always seems to be some set questions people ask. In Boston people want to know what college you went to, even if you graduated decades earlier. And we all know why that is—they just want to know if you went to Harvard or not.

When we lived in Atlanta, new acquaintances would ask, "Where do you worship?" assuming this was a part of our family tradition. Usually I would mention something about Devil Worship just to stir things up. I was raised in a variety of Christian religions—I was baptized Methodist, then we switched to Presbyterians, and for awhile I pretended to be a charismatic Christian due to a crush on an eighth-grade boy (the 6:00 A.M. Bible Studies ruined that relationship). As a freshman at a Lutheran College I learned the Apostles' Creed, and as a 20-year-old I did a quick stint as a Theravada Buddhist while living in Chiang Mai, Thailand. Evan is more Jewish by culture than religion, and together we are raising our kids as Unitarians. You can see the problem when people are looking for the quick answer to the *what-religion-are-you* question. As far as the women in the swim/tennis communities of North Atlanta were concerned—yep, we were Devil Worshippers.

Among the London ex-pat community the questions run in pairs. The first being, "What does your husband do that brings you to London?" To this question I would reply, "Actually, it is my international film career that brought us here. London is so much closer to Mumbai, where I have made quite a name for myself in the Bollywood film industry. My characters are usually chubby European housewives who speak limited Hindi but I always tie my own sari."

After the career question, the next is, "How long do you think you will be in London?" This question is sneaky. It really means, "Should I make an investment in you or not?" If you are with the State Department or an investment firm, the gigs for each country are usually two to three years, and if you are nearing the end of your cycle—heck, why bother pursuing a friendship if that person has one foot out the door? However, if the person is there independently and has been there a while (and perhaps has even become a British citizen)—hey, make the investment and go out for coffee.

And now I am on the plane to San Diego and the man sitting next to me just asked, "So, where do you call home?"

This is probably one of the easiest, most nonthreatening questions you can ask a stranger.

But all I could think was this:

I wish I was back in the U.K. where people don't talk to each other.

I wish I could have an answer that would be brief.

I wish that when he asked me that question it would bring up a mental image of a comfortable house with all our pretty things, linens nicely folded, a fire burning, laughing children, friends gathered around our table.

Instead, an image of the storage facility in Framingham comes to mind.

Instead, an image of the RV parked on the street in St. Louis pops up.

Instead, I feel horrible that we don't have a home for our kids.

But that is not what we tell Josh and Simon. We tell them that home is wherever the four of us are. Walls don't matter. It is about the feeling we create and the love and strength we provide for each other. We have our own family traditions that follow us around, regardless of where we are.

Whose idea is it that "home" has to be a set place?

I feel amazed when I think of the number of places I have called home.

On my bad days I feel like I am a riffraff. A wanderer. Someone not to be trusted because I am a traveler and just passing through. Shifty.

On my good days I feel like an adventurer, a wanderlust, a person who has places to go, people to meet.

I told the man on the plane, "Vermont." Then I smiled nicely and went back to reading my book.

Another Bathroom Floor

San Diego

September 3, 2010

I am sitting on the bathroom floor in the hotel room. I am sharing a room with Garret, my big brother, and I don't want to wake him. He is 51. I am 46. Will I always call him my big brother? While I have left Evan and the boys and the RV in St. Louis, Garret has left his wife and two sons in Palo Alto so we could rendezvous and help move Mom together.

Today is the big day. Bekins Van Lines arrives just after 8:00. We are ready for them. It is a whole different thing helping someone else move as opposed to moving yourself. Not that I usually have too much trouble filling up the boxes to cart off to Goodwill . . . but when it is someone else's stuff, get out the pitchfork!

The things we found:

- The words to songs I wrote while living in Thailand for a farewell dinner with our Chiang Mai University hosts in 1983.

- Medical records from my younger brother's car crash in Yuma, Arizona, in 1985 when he was driving a work truck, fell asleep behind the wheel, and woke up covered in floor wax when he drove off the road.

- The title to an insurance policy from the first house Mom bought by herself in San Diego after she and my dad divorced in 1973.

- Poems and cards written to her by children, grandchildren, friends. Miniature time capsules that transport us to another time and dimension.

I am so glad she is sitting next to me and my brother while we do this. To laugh together. To remember together. To keep the choice pieces and throw the rest in the recycle bins together.

Yesterday Mom had an Open House so her friends could come and pick over what she was getting rid of and have a bit of her with them after she moves. I loved the comments they made to me on the sly, out of earshot of my mom. "I don't know what we are going to do without Jo Anne. She is so positive." "She is the one who holds us together." "She is so much fun and funny." "She is the rock." "She is the one who connects us and keeps us on track and looking forward to new things."

That is my mom.

I am so proud of my mom. She is so accomplished. So fun and funny. So wise. She is a healer. She is a giver. So intuitive. So able to grasp any situation and find the best pieces. She is calling the retirement community in Scottsdale where she is moving her "camp." She has lived in San Diego for 34 years but isn't sad to be leaving. She is looking forward to making new friends and exploring a new place.

What she is sad about is that she isn't able to help me and my brothers anymore. But I don't think that's true. Maybe it's correct physically, because her arthritis is so nasty her hands have turned into claws. But she gives me so many things every day. Mostly, her outlook.

While she is homeless for the next few months before her new place in Scottsdale is available, I am homeless, by choice, in the RV. We are both being flexible, putting ourselves into new situations, and looking forward to the adventure.

I hope I can channel my mom on my bad days to remind myself that life is filled with adventure and that every day is a choice on how you approach it. Yes, it sounds sappy, but it works.

Coming Back to Springfield

Springfield, IL

September 9, 2009

Mom is moved out of her condo, all her things are in storage, and we made it back to join Evan and the boys here in Springfield, Illinois. Whew.

Where am I?

I never lived in Springfield, but I have been coming back here since I was a baby. My mom was born and raised here along with her two sisters and her brother. All Springfield High School graduates. My great grandfather and great grandmother lived down on 4th and Allen Street. Minnie and Ace Frederick. You can't make up names like that. My grandmother, Evelyn Adele, and her husband, Poppa Al, lived over on Douglas Street for the last 10 years. Mama Dell died last spring at 97 years old. Now there was a woman who knew how to have a good time. She would put a hat on and walk around the block and call it a party.

My wonderful aunt and uncle live in a big house down from Washington Park, and they have embraced the addition of our RV to their driveway. We had a family reunion in the park next to the playground. KFC, pizza, Chex mix, delicious salads, and too many desserts. Heaven. Josh and Simon were astounded by the amount of delicious food and the number of second cousins who were their age—even one with red hair.

I imagine most family reunions are like this, where people gather by generation. The elders gather in a circle of lawn chairs talking about their shared memories. The great aunts and uncles who used to share memories of the Great War and life in the 1930s and 40s have made way for my mom's generation talking about the 1950s and their Capezio flats. My generation is in the bullpen waiting to be called up. What will we talk about? 70s pop music and bellbottoms?

We have toured the new Lincoln Museum, which was fabulous; visited with my other aunt and uncle, who live out in the country; ridden our bicycles through never-ending cornfields and past old farm houses; visited the Frank Lloyd Wright Dana Thomas House; and dreamed about fountains for our new house (wherever that may be). We've found the Mel-O-Cream donut factory; participated in Baskin Robbins Tuesday Family Night specials; and started school for the boys (no small feat!). Josh has made two batches of Heath Bar Crunch Cookies from scratch all by himself, and we have spent lazy afternoons with my mom playing Monopoly and hearing her stories of Springfield in the 1950s.

Today we are off in my uncle's Buick for a 1.5-hour drive north to Peoria to check out a planetarium and see the Peoria Chiefs play in the minor league baseball playoff game. Tomorrow New Salem, Illinois, is on the agenda to tour the re-enactment of life on the prairie during Lincoln's era and for the Bluegrass festival.

Hmmm. Maybe Springfield would be a good place to settle once we are finished with the Big Adventure.

RV Elementary - Opening Day
Springfield, Illinois

September 10, 2009

Dear Interested Parties at the Vermont Department of Education and Elsewhere,

We are glad to report that we held RV Elementary Schools Orientation Session on Sunday morning from 10–12 and both students were present.

Please find below the agenda.

Respectfully submitted by,

Reginald (Reggie) P. Higgenbottom, 6th Grade Head Teacher
Penelope (Penny) Q. Snodgrass, 2nd Grade Head Teacher

Orientation to RV Elementary
I. Welcome and introductions

> - Reginald P. Higgenbottom, 6th Grade Head Teacher
> - Penelope Q. Snodgrass, 2nd Grade Head Teacher

II. Goals

- Keep up with 2nd and 6th grade curriculum (maybe beyond) so next year students slip easily into 3rd and 7th grade.
- Encourage students to be creative and flexible.
- Encourage lively and friendly debate.
- Make learning fun by having fun.

III. School Motto

- CARPE DIEM

IV. School Rules

- Respect each other and all teachers.
- Be prepared.
- Do not ask teachers where supplies are.
- Wear seatbelts when school is moving.
- Only comfortable clothing allowed.

V. Schedule

Date	Time	Place
Sun. 9/6	10–12	Springfield: Dining Room Table (DRT)
Mon. 9/7	9–11	Springfield: DRT
Tues. 9/8	9–11	Springfield: DRT and Park for Bike Race
Wed. 9/9	9–11	Springfield: DRT and Peoria, IL
Thurs. 9/10	9–11	Springfield: DRT and Public Library
Fri. 9/11	*MAMA JO*	
Sat. 9/12	*National Holiday – Penelope's Birthday*	
Sun. 9/13	*Drive Day to Topeka, KS*	
Mon. 9/14	9–12	RV Table: Drive to Boulder, CO
Tues. 9/15	9–12	RV Table: Drive to Wyoming
Wed. 9/16	9–12	RV Table: ???

VI. Getting to Know You Games

VII. Refreshments

VIII. Closing

Birthday Projection
Springfield, Illinois

September 12, 2009

It is my birthday. Very early on my birthday. It is 3:37 in the morning. I am 47. All that really means is that I am three years from turning 50.

Josh has been fretting all week trying to figure out what to get me with no money. I keep telling him to write me a poem or a story. He could sing me a song. How about a day of Excruciatingly Fabulous Behavior? All those ideas went over like lead balloons.

During the past few years in London, we always went to my favorite place for my birthday: Kew Gardens. And last year the four of us had an overnight adventure to Dover after a wonderful birthday lunch with my girlfriends at a pub in Maida Vale.

This year we will get up early (check!) and sneak off to the Lincoln Memorial Gardens, where my grandmother's ashes were scattered and my aunt has spent thousands of hours doing everything from fundraising to running the store. It will be lovely.

My 20th birthday I was in Japan on a two week stop over before heading to Chaing Mai University in Thailand where I spent a semester studying Buddhism, SE Asian history and how to make a delicious pad thai .

My 30th birthday I was on the equator in Kenya in the midst of a six-month adventure around the world.

My 40th birthday I had little babies and was living in Georgia.

Projection:

My 50th birthday I will have been living in an RV for the previous three years. My uncut hair will be to my waist; Evan's beard will be to his. Our 10- and 15-year-old boys will be wearing clothes we fashioned from an assortment of indigenous materials we found here in Peru, where the RV broke down (it's up on blocks).

I will have changed my name to Meriwether and the whiskey will be long gone.

Major League Freak-out #3

Springfield, Illinois

September 14, 2009

Here I am again. 2:45 A.M. Awake. No, I don't think it is menopause, nor a panic attack. I think I am just nervous about heading out. For the past 1.5 weeks we have been lounging around my aunt and uncle's beautiful home. We are spread out over the dining room table, the kitchen table, the sun porch, the laundry room, the bathrooms, the bedrooms—heck, our bikes and helmets are all in the garage. We have moved in.

The boys have ridden around the park and know a variety of ways to get to the playground. We have been to Family Night at Baskin Robbins two times, the public library on 7th Street once. All three guys got their haircut at the same barber shop my grandfather used to go to. 12 bucks a head. Josh, the CFO, was not happy. I have been to Schnucks (the grocery store) so many times I know my way around and even have a Loyalty Card.

We were in Peoria at the minor league baseball game Wednesday night watching the Cedar Rapid (that is in Iowa, folks) Kernels play the Peoria Chiefs. Words I am amazed I heard out of my 12-year-old's mouth: "Dad, can we please, please, please go to Cedar Rapids to watch the next game?"

And tonight we were at a bluegrass festival in New Salem with my other aunt and uncle on a perfect late-summer evening. Bluegrass Gospel. Who knew there were so many songs about Calvary and The Old Cross? Jesus is everywhere here in the U.S. of A.

And now we are leaving. Again.

I feel like a truck driver.

Evan has been making soups and freezing them in anticipation of the remote national parks we will be in and the lack of reasonably priced groceries. Tomorrow I have some pumpkin breads to make. I know this is ridiculous but after reading Stephen Ambrose's *Undaunted Courage* and seeing the first half of Ken Burns' *Lewis & Clark*, it seems like we are preparing our 29-foot flat-bottom boat for our own trip. I gotta remember to load on the barrel of whiskey to make sure we can give all our men their daily ration of 1 dram a piece. Maybe that is what I need to get back to sleep.

Sunday we drop Mom at the airport in St. Louis and head to Topeka, then on to Boulder, then to Wyoming.

That's it!

I am freaking out because we are going to Wyoming.

Behind the Wheel

The name sounds like what it is. Faraway. Windswept. Whyyyy? Ohhhhhh! Miiiing! Lonesome. I know in my rational state that all will be well. We will be in the RV for the next two weeks solid and then be in Minneapolis again staying with friends.

That is another cause of my angst. It isn't just the thought of Wyoming; it is knowing we will be in the RV for two weeks straight. Will I have to actually use the toilet in the RV this time? So far I have been able to avoid it.

Relax Wendy. All will be well. Yoga breath.

Nope, that didn't work.

Maybe a few more yoga breaths.

Fill the lungs. Slowly release the breath.

A quiet mind.

That is what I need.

How do you get a quiet mind at 3:08 in the morning?

Is it possible to freak out about your inability to quiet your mind?

Sometimes I fantasize about a partial lobotomy to remove my anxiety lobe. Maybe there is a kit I can get somewhere online. A DIY Lobotomy Kit available on eBay.

Did Meriwether Lewis ever freak out? With a goofy first name like that, I am sure he did. The Lewis and Clark scholars say he was bipolar, which would account for the number of lapses in his journal. But he was driven. And now I am thinking, "I am just having a Meriwether moment."

I need to head back to bed and think about transferring all my anxieties to little puffy white clouds and let them float away.

Yoga breaths. Shots of whiskey. A partial lobotomy. Puffy clouds.

Goodnight, Meriwether.

Small Women and Big Rigs

Somewhere in Kansas

September 14, 2009

I am back behind the wheel.

I love driving the Big Pig. It makes me feel powerful. I am 5 feet, 3 inches tall; the rig is 29 feet long. When I drive I can kind of hear Evan talking to me from the shotgun seat but certainly not the kids' conversation at the table behind me. But I can hear the iPod playing through the front speakers my favorite John Denver, Carole King, and James Taylor tunes, and I can hear myself singing along . . . sounding fabulous I might add. And I can hear and feel the roar of the mighty Ford engine.

I like to pretend I am a truck driver and give a knowing wave to my fellow drivers as I pass. I think I need a hat to be taken more seriously. The two-inch ponytail at the back of my head does a number on the serious factor.

I like driving 15,000 pounds of metal because I get immediate respect from all the little tin cans around me. *Respect* may not be the right word. *Fear*. They know I can do a lot more damage to them than they could ever possibly do to me. Fear because they think I don't know what I am doing and I may go out of control and sideswipe them. Fear because they don't know for sure if I can see them cowering in the right-turn lane. Those little sissies. Hee hee hee.

All of my senses are awake when I am behind the wheel. They have to be. Whenever an 18-wheeler passes on the left the sway blows the Big Pig, and I need to compensate so we don't go over on the shoulder. While we had a few people respond to the Name the RV contest – for some reason Big Pig just seems to fit like a pair of big comfortable jammie bottoms.

Is this love of power and heavy machinery a short-person thing? If I were used to having people look up at me, would I derive as much enjoyment as I do now?

Is this just another issue about respect? Isn't life all about respect?

While in San Diego helping Mom, I got together with my incredible 23-year-old niece—who also happens to be about my height. She picked me up at 6:40 A.M. in order to make the 7:00 A.M. Sunrise Yoga class she teaches in La Jolla. After our 75-minute session (where I got lots of personal attention to help align my arms into the proper warrior, downward dog, and cobra positions), we got our yoga-approved iced coffees and walked along the beach at La Jolla Shores and talked about lots of things. Including short people and respect.

She is dating a short guy. I married a short guy. I have given birth to a couple of short guys . . . although the committee is still out given their ages and we are hoping to channel the Uncle Rick gene, my 6-foot, 2-inch brother. We decided it is definitely harder to be a short guy than a short woman. Society. It all comes back to society. People have preconceived ideas about short people. And it is harder to be taken seriously. So that leads to a few of these options: develop a Napoleonic complex and the need to overcompensate; play the silly one and make it work for you; ignore the whole thing because it is more about who you are—and the more comfortable you are in yourself, the less it matters.

My best friend from college, Becky, is tall: 5 feet, 11 inches. I thought of us as the same height. Then one night coming back from a bar in Northfield, MN, and making the mile walk back up the hill, we passed a storefront with a glass window that acted as a mirror. After years of friendship I finally saw it. I didn't even come up to her shoulder. How could she have respect for someone who didn't even come up to her shoulder? For me, that would be a nine-year-old kid.

I am short and I am proud. Plus nobody knows how tall you are when you are behind the wheel of an RV.

All Wound Up

Outside Cawker City, Kansas

September 15, 2009

We are tooling down Route 24 in Kansas, one of the big square states in the middle of America. Cawker City is in the rearview mirror; Colby is 120 miles in front of us. That is where the nearest Walmart is waiting for us to boondock tonight. [*boon* dock:* to camp overnight for free; usually in the boondocks, a.k.a "the boonies," far away from civilization.]

Walmart is boondocker friendly; in fact, they court us. They are hoping RVers will pull in and have a yearning for a new water filter, a box of Froot Loops, or a round of ammunition at 3:00 A.M. Please note, we are not staying in any old Walmart—we have standards, you know. This is a Super Walmart!

We went to Cawker City, Kansas, because it is home to the world's largest ball of TWINE. We planned our day around the visit.

We needed to go to Cawker City because we are also going to visit the home of the world's largest ball of STRING in Darwin, Minnesota, and we needed to get the good info so we can compare and contrast.

Twine vs string.

Funny how your set of needs can change.

There was a time when I needed to go to Starbucks.
I needed to go to the Parents' Open House Night at the kids' school.
I needed to go to meetings.
I needed to answer emails and phone calls.
I needed to go to the grocery store.
I needed to go to the dry cleaners, the bank, the shoe repair, the library, my office.

What did I need to do today?

Visit a ball of twine.

Miss my old needs? I'm a frayed knot.

On Being Seven Years Old

Grand Teton National Park, Wyoming

September 20, 2009

When I was seven years old, I ran away from home. I was so tired of always having to fight the competition for attention. The competition was fierce: three brothers, a big dog, a couple of cats all vying for the attention of my single mom. But if I ran away, people would notice I was gone and boy would they be sorry. I bet they would have to call the police and everything.

I took my suitcase and packed it with the essentials: cookies I stole from the kitchen, my favorite baby doll, Annie, and a pair of underpants. I put on my coat and walked out the door. 4:00 P.M. on a January afternoon in Minneapolis. Cold, icy, and dark. "Bad idea, Never mind. I will just go and hide in the cleaning closet and that way I will be able to hear everyone talking about me and how worried they are," I thought to myself.

I snuck into the closet. Not a big place, but it had an overhead light you could turn on by pulling a string. This is where all the extra rolls of paper towels, cleaning supplies, the vacuum, and brooms were kept. I could push things to the side and make a little nest from my coat and sit down. For the next hour I played with my doll, ate the cookies, and tidied up the cleaning closet.

An hour later my mom opened up the closest and was surprised to see me. She asked what I was doing in there and I told her, through my tears, "I ran away and nobody even noticed I was gone."

I recently told this story to my boys as we were tooling along the vast expanse of prairie in between Rocky Mountain National Park and our next stop for the night, the Walmart in Rocky Springs, Wyoming. Josh asked Evan and me to tell him "five small moment stories" from our lives. He will be choosing one to expand upon for a writing class he is doing online through Johns Hopkins Center for Talented Youth.

After I told this story, Simon said, "Oh Mommy, I am so sorry for the little girl Wendy. That is exactly how I feel. Nobody talks to me. Nobody plays games with me. Everybody ignores me."

My heart was breaking. "Oh Simon, that isn't right," I replied, and immediately felt guilty for pulling him away from other kids his age. I started thinking this is the issue that is going to get him onto a therapist's couch at the ripe old age of 10.

We decided the next day would be Simon's Day and we would all turn ourselves into seven-year-olds for the day and play. Just play.

Monopoly, card games, book reading, picture drawing, and playing imaginary games. He called me Wendy and we made fun of his teacher Penelope Snodgrass and called her old Stuffy Pants and Antelope Snotgrass. Evan made fun of his teacher old Higgenbottom and we called him Professor HiggenBumBum. We made plans for how we would torment them in our next day of class. But then Simon said Mrs. Snodgrass brought him chocolate crepes for snack one day and that was nice.

For lunch we had a picnic in the City Park in Pineland, Wyoming, where the city motto is "All the civilization you need." We pretended we were airplanes and ninjas and ran around the small pond. We climbed on the big rocks, held hands going double down the slides, swung up to the trees, and climbed to the moon on the climbing frame.

We took an Adventure Walk back into the woods and crossed a bridge, but the bridge was suddenly blown up behind us (so Simon told us) so the only way we could get back across the river was to walk through the water. Simon's croc floated away and Josh came to the rescue and raced through the water, getting all wet but retrieving the croc!

We ate lunch at the picnic table. Simon picked out the menu: mac and cheese and grape Popsicles. We watched each other's tongues turn purple with each lick.

Then I had to go through a portal to turn myself back into a stinky old adult because I needed to drive. But before we went through the portal we made a plan to meet every day to be seven. Excuse me, seven and three quarters.

A Typical Day

Yellowstone National Park, Wyoming

September 23, 2009

Today is Monday—or is it Tuesday?

7:30ish Wake up in Yellowstone National Park (Fishing Bridge Area RV park).

8–8:30 Breakfast in the RV. Cereal, homemade corn muffins, coffee, and juice.

9:00ish RV Elementary.

School begins with Ms. Penelope Snodgrass sitting in for Mr. Higgenbottom, who is busy digging through the basement compartment of the RV looking for warm clothes because it is cold here in Yellowstone. (Alright, it is just a storage space but it feels more spacious to call it a basement.) Mr. Higgenbottom also needs to attend to the backed-up sewer issue, figure out why we are going through so much propane, and apply duct tape to the roof after an unfortunate incident with a low-hanging tree.

School starts as usual with a quote of the day, which elder student hates and thinks is pointless, and younger student hates because he has to write it down in his daily journal and he hates writing.

Today's quote is from George Mathew Allen: "People who live with many interests live not only longest but happiest."

Conversation ensues to discuss interests of said students, which includes the usual suspects of computer games, Lego, robotics, music, reading, and world domination. Discuss importance of being well rounded with lots of interests.

Go through the Junior Ranger packets to see what is required and make sure we take the necessary hikes, explore the habitats of moose, and understand the importance of geothermal hot springs. We have two days to fulfill the requirements, pass the quiz, take the oath, and get the patch.

Note: All U.S. national parks have the Junior Ranger program. The kids are required to fill in an age-appropriate packet or newspaper, attend ranger talks, and do some drawings and reflections. Each park has a unique patch that says Junior Ranger on it that the kids can collect and sew on to their hoodies. Adults can enter the program, too. Yes, I am after my Yellowstone Junior Ranger Patch as well!

10:30 Departure with Mr. Higgenbottom on bicycles to the Mud Volcano to make the 11:00 a.m. ranger talk.

10:45 Realize Mud Volcano site is 7 miles away—uphill on busy road. Too far, too scary. Bike back to RV, unplug electric and water, bring in the slide-out, lock bikes, and head out like proverbial Bats Out of Hell to make 11:00 a.m. ranger talk.

11:02 Arrive at Mud Volcano.

11:04-1:30 Listen to ranger talk and ramble through incredible geothermal mud pots, mud springs, and observe a churning pool of stinky sulfur water endearingly called the Dragon's Mouth. The ranger touchs briefly on the wildlife and the history of the indigenous tribes from the area.

1:40 Drive back the 7 miles to Fishing Bridge Visitor Center.

2-2:45 Make lunch in RV and have picnic at Visitor Center overlooking Lake Yellowstone. Lunch: quesadillas, grapes, yogurt.

3-4:30 Simon and Ms. Snodgrass continue school at Visitor Center. Subjects covered: Music and Art. Listen to headphones in Visitor Center of violin concerto written for Yellowstone. Write stories and draw pictures that are inspired by music. Look at diorama of grizzly bears and draw their picture. Read children's book about the origin of the real Smokey the Bear.

Sit by lake and play the recorder. Or at least try.

MEANWHILE

3-4:30 Josh and Mr. Higgenbottom take the RV to continue school at Merry's Bay, about five miles down the road, where the BlackBerry can pick up a phone tower signal and then convert it to the Internet on the computer so Josh can do some of his online homeschooling.

4:30-6:30 Fill up on propane at the camp store and do laundry at the camp Laundromat.

6:30-7 Make dinner. Boys ride bikes, play in woods, play with balls, read books, complain about how they don't like living in an RV.

7-8:30 Wash dishes, shower.

8:30-9:30 Watch The Waltons on TV in RV.

10:00 Goodnight, John-Boy.

This Is So NOT a Vacation

Yellowstone National Park, Wyoming

September 26, 2009

Can we be clear here? This thing we are doing—living in an RV—is no vacation. We are not waking up each morning wondering if we should go swimming or play croquet.

We do not send our laundry out.

We are not drinking gin and tonics watching the sun set over the Rockies.

But we could. And on second thought—we should!

But this is a lot tougher than I ever imagined. Not that it is all bad, mind you, but we are running a household and being school teachers, companions, and parents in a tiny space. Of course, to quote Simon, "We have a little house, but the whole world is our garden."

All the stuff we dealt with in terms of parenting and chores are still with us. Parenthood: you can run but you can't hide.

This morning's conversation was about allowances. We had previously decided that allowances would be suspended during the RV trip, but there has been a mutiny among the troops. The proposal on the table, as presented by Counselor/CFO Josh, would be for Josh to get $4 a week and Simon $3. $7 a week. That means $1 a day less from the family budget of $110/day.

I thought that sounded a bit extravagant. What do they need to spend all that money on each week? I thought after getting rid of bags and bags of useless plastic objects when we moved out of London it had made an impact on their desire for buying stuff. Are the kids embracing their inner American Consumer?

The boys said they needed that money in order to save up for Christmas gifts for us. Here is the dilemma: Do we give our kids money so they can save it to give it back to us in the form of Christmas gifts?

We decided that Josh would get $2 a week and Simon $1.50 in cash, and that the remaining $2 and $1.50 would go into a Christmas savings account that they would get in a lump sum the first week of December. The money could be used to buy each other gifts. We will play it by ear and see how it works out.

I need a vacation from this adventure . . .

Before we got to Yellowstone, we were in Grand Teton National Park, where they have a great Urgent Care. This is the second Urgent Care we have been to in two months. Simon has strep throat, so we now have a 10-day supply of Amoxicillin in the fridge.

Real-life skills we have taught the kids in the last month:

- How Laundromats work.
- How to budget.
- How to make Ramen noodles into a meal with added vegetables and chicken.
- How to dry dishes.
- How to use a bike lock.
- How to tie shoes.
- How speedometers and odometers work.
- The difference between gas and propane.
- And most important, how to take a shower with very little water.

Here is our Shower Ritual:

1. Remove bag of dirty laundry that is stored in shower stall. Put on bed.
2. Remove laundry basket full of cleaning supplies, bags of potatoes, onions, and apples. Put on bed.
3. Open bathroom door so it swings back for privacy from kitchen and rest of RV and gives you an extra 2 feet of room to remove clothes.
4. Adjust water.
5. Get wet.
6. Turn off water.
7. Soap up.
8. Turn on water and rinse off.
9. Dry shower stall with dirty t-shirt.
10. Get dressed in tiny space.
11. Put stuff back.

But the shower does work. We do get clean. And at this campground there is a water hookup so we can have as much water as we want!

Is it worth it? Well, the highs are high—like right now. It is 6:30 A.M. Simon is asleep. Evan and Josh just left to ride bikes in the dark to the Fishing Bridge Visitor Center to meet up with a group for a five-hour class on Wildlife Photography. Simon—assuming he feels better—and I will have breakfast, do a little schoolwork, work on his Junior Ranger badge, and take a bike ride through unparalleled beauty.

So while this is not a vacation, it is an adventure. Get over yourself, Wendy—it is so not about the shower.

Tomorrow, onward to Devils Tower.

Does My Butt Look Big in This RV?

Somewhere in Eastern Wyoming . . .

September 30, 2009

In July 2007, using data from the Framingham Heart Study, an article by Nicholas Christakis and James Fowler appeared in the *New England Journal of Medicine* stating that one of the strongest indicators of obesity is not lack of physical activity, nor genetics, nor education.

It's your peer group.

If your girlfriends are packing on an extra 40 pounds, then chances are you are in the dressing room next to them at the Pretty and Plump looking at size 24s.

However, if your best buddies are chowing down on carrot sticks, then chances are you are sharing the bag with them while you take your daily walk.

So what do I see as I look around at my fellow RVers—in the Walmart parking lot last night in Rapid City or the KOA here in Interior, South Dakota (population 76)?

This past week, three separate friends emailed the latest photo montage making the Internet rounds. It's called "The People of Walmart." Are these now My People? My peer group?

While the cross-dresser in his four-inch-high, yellow go-go boots looked quite thin, and the guy in cowboy boots and pink velour workout pants was doing pretty well, the women were a mess. Rolls. I am talking rolls on top of rolls. I am talking stretched out stretch pants.

If I am to believe this study, expandable waistline polyester slacks are in my future.

Ok, so I know that these folks, whom we are randomly parked next to for the night, are not my peer group. But just in case, I am taking control!

No fun-size bags of Reese's Peanut Butter Cups for the RV. Bunny-Luv carrots and water rule!

Roll over. Roll on.

Coming to Grips with My Minnesota Nice

Northfield, Minnesota

October 7, 2009

Here we are in Minnesota. We snuck in through the southwest corner along highway 90 from South Dakota. But then we quickly took a right-hand turn and ended up in Spirit Lake, Iowa, for the night, camping along the lake shore at an Iowa State Park. Close enough? Heck no! Iowa is not Minnesota, thank you very much!

However, Spirit Lake was beautiful, and the smells of autumn were everywhere. The fallen leaves, mixed with the smell of the freshwater lake with a hint of a stinky dead Walleye, brought back memories of a life in Minnesota I had forgotten about for decades.

The next day it was back in the Big Pig heading north along a dirt road through harvested cornfields to pop out back in Minnesota again.

What is it about this state that just feels so comfortable? I was born in Minneapolis and lived here until I was 12. Then I returned for college. It just feels like an old comfortable pair of shoes. And isn't that what we all are in search of? Good conversation, a strong cup of coffee, and comfortable shoes?

There is something called Minnesota Nice, and if you have ever met anybody from Minnesota, then you know what I am talking about. That voice over the phone when you know the other person is smiling. The way the lilt in the voice goes up at the end of a sentence. The hint of a smile. The wry sense of humor. Good, down to earth people. Mostly over 6 feet tall, blonde, and with large rear ends.

Passing the towns of Blue Earth and Albert Lea we then turned north to head up Highway 35 to Northfield. You might be thinking to yourself, "Why does that town sound so familiar?" And slowly it comes back. Shootout. Younger brothers. Jesse James. Brad Pitt. Yes! It is where Jesse James and his gang had their last bank robbery attempt thwarted by a band of Swedish and Norwegian townspeople (Q: What do you call a mixed marriage in Minnesota? A: When a Swede marries a Norwegian) and the bank clerk Joseph Lee Heywood, who refused to give up the goods!

Fast-forward a good 100 years. Northfield's motto is now Cows, Colleges, and Contentment. Northfield is home of the most celebrated Norwegian Lutheran college in the world: St. Olaf.

I am neither Norwegian nor Lutheran. But did I ever want to be both during my freshman year at St. Olaf. I mouthed along with the Lutheran Apostles' Creed and ate my leftse and fruktsuppe (fruit soup) with the best of 'em. You betcha! But never the lutefisk. God forbid! Not the lutefisk (raw fish soaked in lye). Each Passover the gefilte fish reminds me of it . . .

I called ahead to arrange a tour of St. Olaf because I knew it had changed quite a bit in the 25 years since I had been there. We were met at the Admission Office by the lovely Amy, a sophomore, from Claremont, CA. Already I knew something was up. She had brown hair.

Turns out she had read about St. Olaf in a handbook called *Colleges That Change Lives*. The college I went to 25 years ago had disappeared and in its place was a much cooler—dare I say edgy?—place with great art installations, inspiring architecture, and the feeling of student involvement everywhere. While I attribute St. Olaf with giving me a fine education and introducing me to a global vision of the world, it always felt like a black spot on my resume. Living in Boston, where everyone asks you in the first 10 minutes where you went to college, saying "St. Olaf" was always met with a wry smile, a comment about Betty White and *The Golden Girls*, and a dismissal that there was no intellectual life west of the New York boarder. But no more—I am embracing my inner Olaf!

From Northfield it was up to Eagan, Minnesota, to stay for six nights with the most hospitable Barb, whom I went to St. Olaf with and shared an apartment in Boston and her fabulous husband Scott, their two daughters, and their two dogs in their beautiful spacious house! What a treat!

I did 29 loads of wash. I showered two times a day because I could. I did somersaults in their living room. Simon and I rolled all over the house with their dogs and we didn't bump into anything.

There were doors! What a great invention.

After two weeks nonstop in the RV, I have a newfound appreciation for the mundane.

We also spent a wonderful afternoon at the Bakken Museum in the old Cornelius House along Lake Calhoun. When I was growing up, the Cornelius Family house was known far and wide because they gave away full-size candy bars at Halloween. But now it is a cool museum devoted to how electricity interacts with human bodies . . . think Frankenstein. Think pacemakers.

After six wonderful days playing with friends and family and renewing ties that were never broken but felt wonderful to retie and hold in my hands, we left yesterday.

But-cha-know, I'm a Minnesota girl. I love claiming it as my home. I love the accents, the beer, the Tater Tots hot dish, the alphabetical street names from Aldrich to Zenith, Garrison Keillor, the huge oak trees that arch over the streets, wild rice, and the plaster cast replicas of Paul Bunyan.

Ya know, I guy could learn a thing or two from the nice people of Minnesota.

Bye now.

Notes from a Moronic Hippie

Manitoba, Canada

October 8, 2009

Have I mentioned we live in a 29-foot RV? Have I mentioned my older son is now my height, can pick me up, wants to start his own country, has designed his own religion, and is demanding his own space?

His own space in the RV. I want my own space in the RV, too!

I love this age of 12. I have loved all the ages my kids have been. Just when I think, "I am done. He is launched. Job over." Nope.

Yesterday we drove from Grand Forks, North Dakota, to Winnipeg, Manitoba, and today we are doing the bone-crunching, butt-numbing, 450-mile drive up to Thompson along Route 6. This is the most rural of places I have been since I lived in a mud hut in Sobela, Mali, in West Africa. Thompson, Manitoba, is where the road ends and we get on the train for the last 320 miles to get up to Churchill so we can see the polar bears!

It is 175 miles between towns, and the towns are so sad. Corrugated metal houses with broken-down cars and refrigerators in the front yards.

People drive in the middle of the road along Route 6 to avoid the particularly big potholes on the sides. The road is so flat you can see a good mile in front of you, so when the one other car on the road that day approaches, you have plenty of time to pull over.

Halfway to Thompson and it is 1:30 in the afternoon. The boys have been plugged into iPods watching movies (all educational, of course) and listening to Weird Al since 10:00 A. M. We stop in Grand Rapids for lunch and to move our bodies with a little bike ride along the one road through town along the Saskatchewan River. The only restaurant in town is run by a man from Shanghai, China. When I told him I was in Shanghai in 1982, he said that was the year he was born. I thought he looked familiar.

After lunch we pull the bikes off the back of the RV, grab our helmets from the RV's basement, and take off—ignoring the yells of protest from our almost teenager. "I don't want to go on a bike ride in this moronic town. I am freezing. How can you do this to me? You and Dad are such morons. Where is my free will? You are such hippies! I hate this Jesus-loving town!"

Evan and Simon take off on a bike race through town and I go back to the RV with Josh to dig out gloves and a scarf and to take the blows from today's hormonal rage of independence.

We discuss what a hippie is. Josh describes a hippie as "Someone who brings their own snacks to public events." I try not to laugh. He tries not to laugh. I suggest that bringing your own snacks is just good planning from an economic and health standpoint. He calls me a hippie again with such disgust it's like a swear word, and when he spits the words out of his mouth, it's like he left a bunch of dirt all over my face.

But he doesn't ride off. He wants to talk. He wants to get me going. He wants a real discussion. He wants a sparring partner. He wants a reaction.

So I give him one.

I says to the guy, I says, "When I think of a hippie I think of someone who goes against the grain: a counterculture type. Hippies are people who march or skip or hop to the tune of their own drummer. I will take this as a compliment and will wear the sobriquet as a badge of honor."

"When I grow up I am going to buy a ranch in California and declare it my own country and I won't pay taxes to this insane American government," says Josh.

"And when you grow up and they take you off to the Federal Pen for tax evasion, I will visit you every Sunday and bring you handmade striped shirts," I reply in a loving, syrupy voice.

I am reminded of the book *The Runaway Bunny* that we used to read when he was three years old about the renegade baby bunny who wanted to make his own way in the world, leaving his mother behind. But wherever he went his mother followed.

Too bad I can't just give Josh a carrot and everything will be better.

Yes, it is hard to be 12. . . . And yes, it is hard to have embarrassing parents.

But Josh, if you are reading this, isn't it better to be embarrassed by your parents in Grand Rapids, Manitoba, where you don't know anyone than at a Middle School in Anytown, U.S.A? Hmmm, next year I think we will park the RV outside your new school and paint it with peace signs with a big banner reading, "We are Josh's parents and we are moronic hippies!"

If we aren't embarrassing our children, we aren't doing our job!

Churchill, Manitoba: Worth the Schlep

Churchill, Manitoba

October 13, 2009

I have never been to a town I have never wanted to live in more than Churchill, Manitoba. It is mid-October and the snow is already on the ground, the wind is whipping off the Hudson Bay at 40 mph, and the architecture is doublewide mobile homes. The tundra is vast and flat with little to break up the scenery other than the leftover rocket silos from a forgotten mission of the U.S. during the Cold War; the abandoned dreams of a man who was building a Rock Castle; and the Bear Jail. The Bear Jail is a corrugated metal Quonset hut where they put errant polar bears that are found walking around town tipping over trash bins.

The tourism industry is what brings in the business to Churchill. Beluga whales in June and July, polar bears in October, and the aurora borealis from November through March. Reason enough to warrant the 10-hour drive from Winnipeg to Thompson—where the road ends—and then the 18-hour train to Churchill?

Even with these negatives the answer is a resounding "yes." Go to Churchill.

What are the options to get to Churchill if there is no road? A quick direct flight from Winnipeg will put you back close to $1,000 a person. Or there is the train. Eighteen-hour travel time compared to two hours by air, but only $200 a person. There are sleeper cars on the train available for an extra $400 per person—but we didn't even think of forking over $1,600 for the four of us, which is the equivalent of two weeks on the road in the RV. But boy oh boy, my 47-year-old body is in the midst of a slow recovery after sleeping sideways on the train's bed of nails.

Back in London last April, Evan booked us for the last four seats available to go out and see the polar bears on Monday. So we booked a dog sledding adventure for Sunday, as one does. At 1:00 on Sunday afternoon we were picked up by the lovely Jennifer from Blue Sky Dog Sleds, who gave us a running commentary of her life in Churchill. Jennifer came to Churchill on a three-week nursing contract seven years ago, went for a dog sled ride, and met her future husband, Gerald—the musher—and she never left. She was a wealth of information and the perfect hostess.

We traveled out from Churchill and parked in front of Blue Sky's permanent tent next to the sign that read "Dog Sled Parking Only—violators will be peed on." There wasn't a poodle or Chihuahua in the mix—all the dogs are gorgeous huskies. Who knew?

Now, I like my dogs as well as the next guy. I grew up with a royal standard poodle, and we are definitely going to get a dog once we are settled and have a yard, but I never would have considered a husky. Until now. What lovely dogs.

I have to say I was a little worried, wondering if this was some sort of animal abuse—I mean, how could dogs be excited to pull fat tourists around in the snow all day? But no, the dogs are all well taken care of, loved, and anxious as anything to be "the chosen ones" to be saddled up to take us for a ride. Since there wasn't enough snow to use the sleigh, they have specially designed carts on wheels so we could still have the experience.

Simon and I were first up for the fastest ride of the day, zipping around on the course through the tundra with the incredibly knowledgeable aforementioned love interest Gerald, the musher, in the driver's seat. Yes, his formal title is The Musher. World Wrestling Foundation take note! Hulk Hogan move over—here comes The Musher.

Dog sledding is remarkably quiet, except for the breathing of the dogs. Watching the backs of the dogs, it was as if they were pulling a feather. The ride was quick, a little scary, definitely dirty—and incredibly memorable.

Afterward we spent time getting to know the other dogs in the yard, including Isobel, the Blind Snow Dog, who still loves to get out there in the pack. We also had a chance to hear Gerald and Jennifer tell us stories over hot chocolate and cake about their life in the Churchill suburbs, where moose, polar bears, and wolves play a pretty regular role. In fact, it is common to hear shots around town as the Bear Police keep the polar bears out of town.

Behind the Wheel

Any bear that is caught in town digging through trash cans is tranquilized and brought to the 24-occupancy, previously mentioned Bear Jail, where they are kept without food (except for water and snow) until the Hudson Bay freezes. The Bear Jail is right on the shores of the Hudson Bay, so the Jailers just open the doors, and the bears run out of the jail and head straight up to the Arctic Circle.

Mushers, Jailers. Arctic Circle. Tundra. These are not words I use very often yet they are all part of a regular ol' day here in Churchill.

On Monday we were off on the Tundra Buggy—a cross between a school bus and a Hummer, only on steroids. With tires 6-feet tall, a viewing balcony off the back, seating for 30, and a toilet, a Tundra Buggy can make its way over the rocks, packed ice, and streams that make up the terrain along this southern section of the Hudson Bay. Our guide, Brendon, a Churchill native, had eagle eyes that could spot a polar bear miles away.

Within a few minutes we saw our first polar bear—a three-year-old male—messing about on the rocks. Later we spent a few hours with another very large male, observing him while he napped. Occasionally he would wake up and acknowledge the four Tundra Buggies gathered around him Wagon Train style. Then he would stretch and settle back down for another nap.

I am happy to report that the polar bears are healthy this year due to the late breakup of the ice this past spring. This gave them an extra couple of weeks to fatten up on seal meat before they had their cubs.

It was a funny experience knowing that we were observing polar bears in the wild and that there is a good chance they will become extinct during our lifetime. It was also embarrassing that after the first four hours I started to think, "Goodness, this is getting really boring watching a polar bear nap. We traveled so far to get here and . . . yawn . . ." Yes, I did take a nap myself.

Back in town that afternoon I wondered, "What's it like for the 942 people who live here year-round?" I made my way over to Churchill's Frontier School, grades K through 12, which doubles as a Community Center where the adult swim is held from 5:00–7:00 P.M. As I was walking in I saw large posters on the wall announcing the finding from the Sustainability Study that was conducted by the University of Winnipeg along with the Churchill community. One of the things that struck me was the list of hazards to the citizens of Churchill: high winds, tornados, draughts, floods, snow, hail, ice storms, fog, polar bears, and chemical contamination from the ports. Certainly not the type of note put up by anyone hoping to sell homes.

I wandered around the Community Center, following the smell of chlorine to find the pool down in the basement. There were no other swimmers there, just a bored young woman who took my 50-cent entrance fee. Once I had suited up in the locker room and made my way to the pool, she had to move down from the office into the wet area to be there to save me in case I drowned. Phew. I was worried.

After about 15 minutes of laps I picked my head up and saw she had two friends sitting with her—a boy and a girl. Now I really felt secure. Three people watching me drag myself through the pool making sure I was breathing.

After about 30 minutes I pulled myself out of the pool, wrapped up in my towel, said my thank-yous, and asked the three of them, "So, do you go to high school here?" They all nodded their heads. I then asked, "So, what is it like to live in Churchill?" Without missing a beat they all said, in chorus, "Bor - ing!" All three were hoping to move to Winnipeg upon graduation. Only one had ever been to Winnipeg before—he took the train.

I am having trouble getting my head around Northern Canada. The loneliness, the barren tundra, the nomadic culture, the houses up on blocks. But I do have an incredible respect for the people who live here and the challenges they must face.

But I am so not interested in dropping by the local real estate agent to see what is on the market.

Schadenfreude

Grand Forks, North Dakota

October 22, 2009

According to Dictionary.com "Schadenfreude" is the malicious joy in the misfortunes of others," 1922, from Ger., lit. "damage-joy," from schaden "damage, harm, injury" + freude, "joy," "happy," literally "hopping for joy."

I love this word. I love the naughty, guilty pleasure I get when I feel a pang of schadenfreude. Perhaps you will feel this way after you read the following. Don't feel guilty! You have my complete blessing. Know that I am laughing with you.

Imagine if you will: Our 29-foot white Winnebago with the sporty stripe camped in the Walmart parking lot . . . again. This time in Grand Forks, North Dakota.

This is a familiar parking lot. We stayed here just 12 days before on the way up to Churchill, Manitoba, and we liked the neighborhood so much we thought we would drop by on the return trip. Splasher's of the South Seas Water Park is just down the street. The Red Lobster sign shines a nice ruby-red glow in the front window of the RV. And the trees that are planted in the parking lot (in an attempt to disguise the vast parking lot that it really is) are skinny and losing their leaves but appreciated.

Parking Lot, Sweet Parking Lot (if I knew how to embroider, that's what I'd be putting on one of our pillows).

After a nice swim at Splasher's Water Park, a dinner of leftovers, and an exciting game of Clue, we are all snuggled into our beds.

Then at 3:00 A.M. a loud beating of hands against the side of the RV wakes us all up. Funny how we are thousands of years from cavemen but our responses are programmed just the same.

Evan, the protector, wakes up yelling, "Get out of here!"

I, on the other hand, wake up silently, thinking to myself, "If we hide, they will go away."

We hear the drunken voices and laughter of teenagers as they continue their weaving path across the parking lot. We are fine.

Simon makes his way into our bed about 45 seconds later. "What was that noise? I had a bad dream. Can I sleep with you?" We move over.

Josh makes his way back into our bed two minutes later. "The tree branches look like a hand and it's scratching against the window." We move over again.

If we all sleep on our sides we fit, but nobody sleeps.

I contort my body so I can climb out of there.

Are we seeing the humor in this, people? We have a queen-size bed in the back of an RV with a family of four all sleeping together in the Walmart parking lot in Grand Forks, North Dakota, for god sakes!

It is 3:00 A.M. and I am in my fashionable flannel Target gnome pajamas crawling through arms and legs and twisted blankets in a room no bigger than the bed.

I make my way to the front of the RV to sleep on Simon's pull-out couch, where he has been sleeping since Josh threw him out of the queen-size bed above the cab way back in Wyoming. But here I will have a little more room, in order to go back to sleep.

Sleep. Yeah, right. 3:00 A.M. Awakened by hooligans. Who am I kidding? I am not sleeping. I am lying wide awake in the RV making lists of what to worry about next.

1. Carbon monoxide poisoning. We will be found by the Walmart Greeter three days from now when the 48-hour RV parking limit is up.

2. It is cold outside. The gray-and-black water in the RV holding tank will freeze, the pipes will burst, and an ugly stinking rain will pour down around the RV.

3. We will run out of propane and freeze to death.

4. The gang of skinny, pimply-faced Grand Forks teenagers will return to finish the job.

5. Josh and Simon will be scarred for life due to the RV trip, they will never get jobs, and they will live at home forever, hating us the whole time.

6. Even worse—Josh and Simon will decide they love being homeschooled and taking RV trips and this will be my life forever.

I hear the tree scraping against the small window that Josh mentioned. Yep, it is scary. I peek through the window to make sure the bad guys have left. Nothing out there but a vacant parking lot. Still, I put my cell phone and keys right next to my pillow so I am ready for a quick getaway.

I make a mental note to explore over-the-counter, organic, nonaddictive sleeping-aid options in the morning at the Walmart pharmacy.

I finally fall asleep.

Pajama Talk

Zumbro Falls, Minnesota

October 29, 2009

We need to talk about pajamas. I don't mean nightshirts, nightgowns, or boxers and t-shirts; I mean two-piece pajamas—usually flannel—with either a drawstring waist or an elastic one. A button-up top is a given. But not the kind with built-in feet; those are too hard to wear when you are driving a car, especially the kind with the little plastic bumps on the soles.

My mother has accused me of wearing my pajamas a little too often. I have been known to get into my pajamas far before bedtime and to stay in them well past noon. I have cooked meals in them, gardened in them, walked to the end of the driveway to pick up a poorly tossed newspaper, and on our first Christmas in London, I went to my next-door neighbor Jane's house in my pajamas and had coffee in a move that cemented our friendship.

And yes, I have thrown a coat and boots on and worn them to the grocery store—but only before 9:00 A.M. Not that there are any set rules and regulations regarding improprieties and pajama wear like there are with white shoes after Labor Day, but I do have some self-respect.

And then of course there are the Pajama Adventures I have had with my jetlagged kids in various parts of the U.S. when we sneak out of the house or hotel in pajamas and look for trouble (and donuts) between 5:00 and 6:00 A.M.

Everything is a little more fun if you do it in pajamas.

My mom has commented that I am the only person she knows who has worn out pajamas. But considering how much I wear them, that is to be expected.

And then there was last weekend. We were staying with our friends in Zumbro Falls, Minnesota, population 177. Five of those people are my friends Doug and Pam and their three kids. I hadn't seen Pam for 20 years and she still looks 23. We parked the Big Pig in a snowstorm Friday night next to their new house—their new house because the old house was damaged by a tornado.

Saturday morning I walked across the muddy driveway in my pajamas (of course) and boots around 9:00 A.M. to hang out, drink coffee, and have breakfast. I walked in and Doug said, "Did Pam loan you her pajamas?" I was wearing my gnome pajamas. Pam was wearing hers.

There are some friends you don't see for 20 years and those years just dissolve over a cup of coffee in your matching gnome pjs.

Two-timing My Loyalty Cards

Sun Valley, Idaho

November 6, 2009

I am a person you can rely on. I am a good friend. I am the gal who will pick up your kids after school if you are running late, bring them home, feed them home-baked cookies, make up goofy songs on the guitar with them, and make you feel guilty that you aren't as much fun of a mom as I am.

I am the neighbor who plants perennials, sweeps her walk, and talks to everybody who walks by. I am the one who plans the block parties for the street. I am the one who connects people and has the good information. I am the Go-to-Gal and I am proud of it!

I don't think of myself as one of those people who move all the time. Shiftless. Rootless. Not willing to commit. Just passing through.

But now I am facing the ugly reality. My wallet betrays me for what I am. A poser. A shiftless hussy. An opportunist willing to pass herself off to save a buck.

It started off innocently enough back in July in Vermont. Shaw's grocery store in Manchester is the big grocery store in a town with a population of 4180. It is.about a 30-minute drive from the holiday house, so I am there once a week during the four or five weeks we are in Vermont every summer. I had no qualms about signing up for their Loyalty Program. Especially now that I have a permanent address in Vermont, our car has Vermont plates, and I carry a Vermont driving license.

But then I was enticed by the much smaller Price Chopper. Was it their 2-for-1 specials on all boxes of cereal? Their proximity to the one movie theater in town? Did I feel I could connect more with the less polished ambiance and the more true Vermonters who shopped there as opposed to the throngs of summer residents who congregated at Shaw's?

Whatever the reason, I did it. I signed up for their Loyalty Card Program as well. Later, I justified the brief affair by noting that as we were passing through the small towns of western New York, there were a number of Price Choppers where I could use the card as well.

And then there was Schnucks grocery. We were first introduced in St. Louis, Missouri, and kept up our relationship as we moved into Illinois. With an in-house Starbucks, ease in finding parking for the Big Pig, and lovely produce aisles, I was seduced, Writing down my aunt and uncle's address, I held my breath, took the plunge, and signed on the dotted line.

Alright, I am coming clean. The next was just a brief affair. Simon was sick. We were in Boulder, Colorado, and I needed Children's Sudafed to keep his ears clear since we would be driving an additional 2,000 feet up to the Colorado Rockies National Park. I zipped through Safeway while Evan circled the parking lot. I could save $2 on the Sudafed if I became a Safeway Club Member. I am a joiner! I want to be part of the club! I wanted to make our CFO son proud that I was looking for ways to save. I took the form, filled it out as I waited in line, swiped my pristine card at the cash register, and saved the $2. True confession: I never turned the form in. I think it is in a recycling bin in South Dakota.

And now we have landed in Sun Valley, Idaho, for a few weeks of much needed hangout time at a friend's beautiful condo. But my assorted past is catching up to me. After three months on the road and five months of travel I have become calloused and brazen. I rarely flinch when I go to the courtesy window at the local grocery store and request an application. But it is always when you get too confident that you get caught.

In Ketchum, Idaho (population 3,244), the grocery store is Atkinsons'. In Hailey, the next big town, there is an Albertsons. Atkinsons' vs. Albertsons . . . you can see where this is going, yes?

I have all my tricks down for hiding my various Loyalty Cards. God forbid they find out about each other. I have a little pouch in my wallet where I keep them all and pull out the one I need as I approach the cashier. Why do I keep them all? Reminders of past purchases? Past campgrounds? Meals cooked? Forgotten youth?

So there I was at the Atkinsons' checkout holding my Albertsons card up proudly to the cashier. She looked at me and said, "I will have to charge you double with that card."

The shame.
The remorse.
The loss of trust.
The need for forgiveness.
I'm not even Catholic and I am having fantasies about going into a confessional.

Until I fall in love with my next grocery store . . .

Hemingway's Grave

Sun Valley, Idaho

November 11, 2009

When I was 10 years old I went to Marcy Open School in SE Minneapolis and we studied graveyards. Open schools are designed with no set curriculum so students can have the freedom to follow their own passions. At 10 my passions were Laura Ingalls Wilder, pioneer life, math, and graveyards.

Some kids were passionate about pottery and spent the year in the Pottery Shed making ashtrays and mugs. Some kids were passionate about machinery and spent weeks, or months, with Stan the Carpenter in Hammer Hall. I remember one boy was passionate about a square skateboard that he rode unceasingly throughout the entire school, inside, everyday. Ruthie and Lisa were passionate about Marlboro cigarettes and talking about boys. I was passionately scared of Ruthie and Lisa, but I wasn't scared of graveyards.

We studied why people died and which epidemics went through Minnesota from the 1860s through the 1920s, and then we went out in search of those people whose lives were taken so abruptly. One wild weekend we camped in southern Minnesota in the oldest graveyard in the state looking for diphtheria victims. We found entire families taken out by disease and did rubbings of their gravestones. I didn't think of it as weird—rather, we were collecting stories of people whom I wished I could know more about. I often thought, and still think, "Wouldn't it be cool to have a little screen on the gravestone, push a button, and see a video of that person's life?"

My love of cemeteries traveled with me when I moved to Boston and I found myself spending many hours at Mount Auburn Cemetery in Cambridge, MA. Evan and I had a date or two wandering around through the tombs, past the lake looking for birds, and up the tower to look out at the views of Boston across the Charles River. I remember visiting Mount Auburn Cemetery when I was eight months pregnant, scouring the grounds with my aunt and uncle, devoted botanists, in search of the prize-winning beech trees.

Needless to say, here in Ketchum, Idaho, we had to check out Hemingway's grave and pay homage. First we stopped by The Community Library to see if we could get some background material on the man. The Community Library is privately funded and anyone can get a library card. For those of us with no fixed address and a thirst for information, it is a perfect match. It has provided us with a wonderful space for teaching school, it has Wi-Fi throughout, and the librarians are helpful. Librarians. What wonderful people.

Side note: I was so proud of Josh when he mentioned that his favorite store in Ketchum is The Gold Mine—a thrift store whose proceeds benefit The Community Library. Josh shares my view that the best thrift stores are in rich towns and that if you need to buy something, why not buy it at a place that benefits a cause you believe in? Plus, we found a $10 waffle maker there!

In the library we found Sandra, the research librarian who gave an impromptu child-friendly lecture on Hemingway in Ketchum. Next thing you know we are hearing about Hemingway's son Jack, who at the age of eight ran up a $600 tab at the Sun Valley Lodge eating his way through the menu. We discussed famous writers and how just a mere speck of writers can actually make a living off of their passion. We discussed how writers in the 1930s were as famous as rock stars are today and how Sun Valley, as a marketing ploy, enticed Hemingway to come to Sun Valley Lodge to write in exchange for permission to take photos of him enjoying himself. Room 206 is where he finished *For Whom the Bell Tolls*.

With books in hand we made our way 1.5 miles down the road from the library to the graveyard. His grave is very plain. We stumbled on it because it was strewn with empty wine bottles, cigarettes, pens, and pennies. We sat on the grave. We read from *The Old Man and the Sea* and speculated on relationships between old and young people, Cuba, and the fishing trade. We added our own coins and wondered about who the people were who made pilgrimages to his grave.

Too bad we didn't have a flask of whiskey to offer up.

Semi-Affluent Homeless Person

St. Helens, Oregon

November 16, 2009

I was cruising websites the other day and stumbled on an article about an Airstream Rally. Airstreams are high-end RVs. And rallies, as we all know, are when a bunch of people who are wild about something get together to go wild about it en masse so they won't feel so weird about doing it on their own. It's a validation thing. It's a sharing of information thing. It's a genuine geek-out festival.

I have been to rallies. I have organized rallies—albeit for political candidates or causes. But I really hope I never find myself at a rally for an RV.

However, Airstreams really are beautiful, retro silver bullets that remind me of the Jetsons cartoons because they look like what we used to think the future would look like. Only the future is here and we still don't have individual hovercrafts—which really bums me out. Nor do we have those really cool conveyor belts that you can roll onto from bed in the morning in your pajamas and robots automatically wash, polish, and feed you and then zip you into your clothes for the day.

At the Airstream Rally, someone was selling pins that said "Semi-Affluent Homeless Person." According to a number of RV websites and blogs, this is how my family would be designated if the U.S. Census Bureau came knocking on the door of the Big Pig.

When I looked at the U.S. Census Bureau and IRS websites, I found no validation of the term. I think people who are living in their RVs made it up and it has turned into an urban myth . . . or would that be an RV Park Myth?

Full-time RVers like the term because it makes them feel like they are part of a movement. There are so many full-time RVers they have their own designated box to tick on a form from the government. Anyone knows that you are a powerful contingent when you get a box to tick that says what you really are and you don't have to settle for one that just says "Other."

Full-time RVers. They have our own rallies. They have our own pins. They have their own t-shirts. They are organized and they vote. They are a movement. But most important, they have their own cheer:

Hey RVers. Hey RVers.
Introduce yourselves, right on!
Introduce yourselves, right on!
We are RVers . . . and we are proud.

That's why we honk . . . so very loud.
Honk Honk!

Who needs validation from the Federal Government so long as you have
your own cheer?

Being Present

Bend, Oregon

November 19, 2009

I will not obsess that we haven't had a home for five months.

I will not dwell on the fact that neither Evan nor I have jobs.

I will not worry that Simon is not doing 2nd-grade work, has yet to lose a tooth at close to eight years old, and refuses to get his hair cut.

I will not fret that we have no doctors.

I will not give a rat's ass that I dress like a woman who has no fashion sense, showers every other day, and hasn't had a proper haircut in six months.

I will trust that all this will pass and that when we decide to, we will be back amongst society, find jobs, own a house, tend to a garden, wear matching clothes, see doctors, and start bathing regularly.

What I will do now is be aware of and wallow in life's goofiness, its teaching moments, and the chance to be together with my family knowing that all will be well. This trip isn't about having courage, it is about having trust.

Small moments are what make up a life. This is it. Life is short and it can change quickly.

Here are some of my moments over the past few days:

1. Hearing the word *ennui*. Isn't is weird how a word you don't really use comes up, you discuss it, and next thing you know it starts popping up all over the place? The word *ennui* first came up in a book Julia shared with us in Minnesota, where a child dies of a horrible case of *ennui*. It came up again while listening to the Cole Porter song "Anything Goes," and then in the book *Gooney Bird Greene* by Lois Lowry. Gooney Bird is an eccentric seven-year-old girl, and what she does to ward off a dreaded case of ennui is to always wear mismatched socks. Our family embraces this wholeheartedly.

2. Shopping at Trader Joe's in Bend, Oregon, in anticipation of camping the next four nights. I tried their samples. A couple of times.

3. Eating pie at the Starlight Café in Vale, Oregon.

4. Taking an early morning walk with Josh through the ghetto of sad trailers in Vale and discussing the importance of respecting all people—including poor people. The conversation changed to include gangster rap music, hoodies, sunglasses, and how while we are just

passing through the RV/trailer park part of our lives, some other people don't have the luxury of choices.

5. Driving through a snowstorm south of Bend in the dark. I was behind the wheel. Josh was nervous, but he leaned over and told me that he feels more confident when I drive. He added, "How ironic it is, Mom. Dad is the calm, matter-of-fact one and you are the wild-and-crazy one, but when you drive, you reverse roles." He noticed.

6. Showering in a clean bath house. Last night at the Big Pines RV Park in Crescent, Oregon, we were very pleasantly surprised to find a lovely warm, large, and clean bath house. A cozy recreation room separated the men's from the women's showers. Josh and I packed up our shower kits and clean pajamas and headed over in the dark, through the snow banks, under a clear sky full of incredible stars. Simon came with us as our entertainment. He promised jokes. It turned into a joke contest. Since Josh and I couldn't hear each other over the sound of running water, Simon was the interpreter, running back and forth between the showers to tell us each other's latest entry in the competition. The winner? Q: Why did the monkey fall out of the tree? A: Because it was dead.

7. Cuddling with Simon. This morning I woke up to Simon (who had crawled into our bed at some point in the wee hours of the night) asking me, "Mom, do you want to know what my favorite things are?" "Why yes, why don't you tell me," I replied in a gravelly voice. "Eating and sleeping," he said. "Oh, I bet there are some more," I prodded. "Oh yeah, rock climbing, bike riding, my birthday, and cuddling!" he yelled. Then he gave me a full body cuddle.

8. Listening to the quiet. Today we drove to Crater Lake National Park in Oregon. Only the south entrance is open after October. They have already received close to five feet of snow. They have over 15,000 visitors a year. Today we were four of the seven visitors all day. We took a 2-mile gorgeous hike out to Destination Point on snowshoes. On the way back we stopped midway to break off huge icicles and suck on them like Popsicles. We decided they needed a bit of sugar. We stopped again to listen to the quiet. I don't ever remember hearing nothing for so long.

Right now we are tucked in for the night at Jo's Motel & Campground and Organic Grocery & Deli by Crater Lake in Fort Klamath, Oregon. We are listening to Ella Fitzgerald while I write this at the table in the RV. Simon is sitting in the back having some alone time with his container of stuffed animals. Evan is editing the photos from today. Josh is sitting across from me working on a homework assignment, and he is quietly singing along to Ella.

To quote some sappy Holly Hobbie-esque poem that is, however, true . . .

Yesterday is history, tomorrow is a mystery
Today is a gift, that is why it is called "the present."

In Praise of Libraries

Vale, Oregon

November 27, 2009

"Having fun isn't hard, when you've got a library card,"
Arthur the Aardvark

729 Boylston Street, Boston MA 02116. An address I can rattle off in my sleep 15 years after I worked there. On the second floor there was a tailor shop where the three sisters worked, all in their 70s, none of whom had ever married. They had worked in the same 10' x 12' shop since after the war, the big one, WWII, inheriting the business from their father. I employed their services to alter my wedding dress, which I had picked up for $100. It cost me more to have it altered and boy, did they have fun at my expense as I modeled the dress with straight pins sticking into my skin.

I worked on the 5th floor, which also had roof access. This was the place to be on Boston Marathon Day, where we could peer over the edge to see the skinny, sinewy runners crossing the finish line as we ate our bagels and drank coffee.

The office building was nestled between the Pizzeria Uno and Au Bon Pain, where in winter I would buy my salads to eat at my desk, which had a lovely view into a light well where pigeon poop, air conditioning vents, fire escapes, soda lids, cigarettes butts, and old plastic bags would greet me. But on a beautiful day in the spring, summer, or fall, I would take my salad and go into the secret courtyard of the Boston Public Library.

I would enter on the north side under the words of the library's Board of Trustees etched high above: "The Commonwealth requires the education of the people as the safeguard of order and liberty." But I wasn't interested in the education, I was interested in a bit of solace, a safe and quiet space, a free place to sit where no one would bother me, the phone wouldn't ring, and I could read while eating my salad balanced on my lap.

Having sneaky relationships with libraries is an indulgence I have had since I was little, when I would go to the Linden Hills Library in Minneapolis. Upstairs was the adult section, where I learned the meaning of the word *quiet*. Downstairs was the children's section, where I would sit for hours lost in another world and then wake up my legs, put on five layers of clothes, and walk home with my new treasures. All for free! As someone once said, "Knowledge is free at the library—just bring your own container." Unfortunately, while I have no problem finding the bottom of the container, I have trouble finding a lid that fits properly and the knowledge keeps sloshing out. So I keep going back for another fill-up.

At St. Olaf College, my student job was working at Rolvaag Memorial Library, checking out books, shelving books, and—during one ridiculously magical night—tap dancing on the tables once we were closed. At Graduate School at Tufts University, I studied down in the basement in the deathly quiet, rarely used, study carrels until the notorious flasher found me (from then on I studied in the well lit and highly populated reading room).

Once I had kids, I realized libraries weren't just about sneaky spaces and free books; they also served as hubs for the community and provided opportunities to find friends and outlets for stay-at-home moms who were going nuts with their babies. Story time. Sing-along time. Arts-and-crafts time. A place to go. Again, all for free.

In London, the stinky Golders Green Library, with their dirty toys and limited selection of sticky children's board books, had a redeeming grace: It netted me an introduction to Wallace and Gromit, and my dear friend Mei Chen. We had been in London for just a few weeks and the library was a destination for eighteen-month-old Simon, six-year-old Josh, and me. We could walk there, do our shopping along the way, check out books, and stop for a snack as we headed home. On a fateful October 16, 2003, Mei and Justin, her almost two-year-old, were there as well. We chatted, we laughed, we chatted some more, the boys played. By the end of the quick encounter we had exchanged numbers and Simon and I were invited to Justin's birthday party the next day. We have been great friends ever since. Score another win for the library!

Since we have been back in the U.S. we have been using the public libraries as classrooms to homeschool our boys, and as warm places to retreat to on cold rainy days, plug in our computers, use their free Wi-Fi, and explore the books on the shelves in a safe, inviting atmosphere.

From the Mark Skinner Library in Manchester, Vermont, to the Lincoln Library in Springfield, Illinois, to the fabulous libraries in Minneapolis, Minnesota and Great Forks, North Dakota not to mention Thompson, Manitoba and the Ketchum, Idaho Community Library, and now here we are at the Hood River County Library on State Street. We have been borrowing our friends library cards, checking out material and mailing the books back from a destination further down the road. We have also used our time at the libraries to see what is going on in the local communities across the nation. We are happy to report that the libraries are packed with people, opportunity and plenty of ideas.

To paraphrase Lady Bird Johnson, there is no other institution that is more democratic than a town library. The only entrance requirement is interest.

Shut Up and Listen

Hood River, Oregon

December 1, 2009

I have moved a lot and every time I move I think, "This time I will be the quiet, mysterious one. The woman who leaves a lot unsaid. The woman whom people wonder about because she said so little—but what she did say was so intriguing. The woman with the slightly foreign accent wrapped in a scent of sandalwood."

It hasn't worked yet because I talk too much.

Only when I hit the age of 35 did it dawn on me that if you don't tell people things, they don't know. For some reason I still felt compelled to tell everybody, everything, all the time, whether they were interested or not.

Then we moved to the U.K., where it is socially unacceptable to divulge much of anything, ever. Unless you are drunk. You barely nod acknowledgement to people whom you do know as you walk down the street, let alone to a stranger. Then there is the whole protocol when it comes to the morning school run. I had to learn this because I always walked the mile to the Hampstead Garden Suburb Infant School to drop Simon for reception—the U.S. equivalent of preschool. Women, mostly all women, whom I would walk next to everyday under the large arcade would not share a glance, god forbid a smile. After the first term there might be an acknowledging look, after the second term a half smile, toward the end of the year, a slight wave.

On my low self-esteem days I would think, "These women with their posh British accents have all attended Oxford, grown up with Dickens and Shakespeare, and are probably dropping their kids off before they return to their massive 17th-century home libraries to translate Chaucer and they just can't be bothered with the unwashed masses such as myself."

On my better self-esteem days I would think, "This nation is so repressed and stuck in its ridiculous social classes that nobody can acknowledge anyone without a proper introduction. They are missing all the fun in life!"

And then I went out to lunch with an American woman whom a friend from the U.S. had introduced me to. She had just moved to London and was in the market for friendship, information on the city, and the gossip about the local school. I had been living in London for a number of years and I could fill her in. Over the course of our hour-long lunch, she didn't stop talking a second. By the time we asked for the bill, I knew where she was born, her alma mater, her children's learning issues, her professional life, her past relationships, her future travel plans, her morning conversation with her husband, her hopes, her dreams, and her bowel movement patterns.

Profound observation of the absurdly obvious: The more someone else talks, the less you have to talk. And the more this woman talked, the less I wanted to tell her anything about myself. When we said good-bye I felt as if I was walking away from a one-night stand: bowled over, exhausted, and used. I made a promise to myself to never again be as unrelentingly chatty as she was throughout our lunch.

Over the past three months since we have been on the road, I am talking less and less. Given, I don't have as many people to talk to, and the three people I am with are mostly interested in the latest *Heroes* episode, computer role-play games, and Bionicles. But I have also had more time by myself than I have ever had—by myself but not alone.

I am realizing it is ok to be quiet with others in the room. I don't feel compelled to fill up the room with my chatter. And I realize that most of my chatter used to be about the adventures of the day and the people I had encountered. When you live with people 24/7 there are no adventures they don't already know about. And since most of our adventures are of the remote variety, we don't have as many encounters with other people in the course of the day.

I am learning to listen more. As we were snowshoeing for a couple of hours around Crater Lake, we stopped to listen to the quiet. The silence was deafening. Not a bird. No wind. No airplanes. No cars. Just stillness.

When we finally land, maybe this will be the time I finally start speaking with a slight accent, change my name to Elise, and dab myself with sandalwood perfume.

Penelope Snodgrass′ School for Boy(s)

Hood River, Oregon

December 10, 2009

Penelope Snodgrass' School for Boy(s)

Mission: To enlighten young charge to the silliness of life through games, recess, and small chocolate treats whenever possible.

Objective: To keep up with the 2nd-grade curriculum so that repetition of the year is not necessary upon landing back in alternative reality.

Materials used: Every Day Math, Time4Learning website, writing books, blank books, random writing journals, blogs, Junior Ranger programs, road signs, tourist brochures, maps, restaurant menus, sticks, pinecones, stones, money, marshmallows, bits of paper, colored pencils, crayons, needles and thread, old socks, egg cartons, and lots of books.

A typical day:

7:15   Alarm. Ignore.

8:00   Alright already. Out of bed.

8:15-8:45   Cooking class. Banana chocolate chip muffins. Review fractions by doubling the recipe. ½ tsp +1/2 tsp =1 tsp of baking soda. More important, whenever given the option of ½ cup vs. 1 cup of chocolate chips, go for the 1 cup. Sample chocolate chips to ensure they are not poisonous.

8:45   Breakfast. Bacon and scrambled eggs. Hot chocolate if possible. Whipped cream if available. Sample whipped cream if in a canister directly into mouth for sanitary purposes.

9:00   School starts. Strictness about timing is crucial. Kind of.

Today's schedule:

9:03-9:10   Day book. Fill in first new clean page with: date, where we happen to be that day, and the day's activities. Sometimes includes a quote of the day depending on creativity, organizational skills, and preparedness of Ms. Snodgrass.

9:10-9:30   Write postcards to four best friends. Three in London. One in Connecticut. Discuss how much we miss them. What are they doing now?

9:30-9:45   Clean out and reorganize pencil box and traveling milk crate.

9:45-10:45   Research fun things to do in Seattle. Times open. Cost. Café and gift shop availability. Proximity to public transportation or parking for Big Pig. Zoos are always good.

10:45–11:05   Card game! 21 . . . with chips. Ms. Snodgrass is reminded of Willie Nelson song "The Gambler." Pulls out guitar, finds words and music. Impromptu music class. Discussion of metaphor "I see you are out of aces" and Simon's middle name—Ace. Make connections between whiskey-swilling, cigarette-smoking gamblers and seven-year-olds. No real whiskey is involved.

11:05-11:45   Everyday Math. Knock off six pages. Review digital and analogue clocks with the help of our Marshmallow Clock and homemade flash cards for a matching game. Ms. Snodgrass loses . . . again.

11:45-1:00   Bike ride hitting following spots:

1. Post office to mail postcards written in the A.M. Discuss postal system, stamps. Price variance between U.S. and U.K. stamps. Stamp design.

2. Hood River Waterfront Playground. Practice climbing techniques picked up at the Sun Valley YMCA. No, Ms. Snodgrass will not be joining her class on the top of the structure even though she does realize the view of the Columbia River Gorge is even better from the higher vantage point. Yes, of course Ms. Snodgrass could mount the wall in a matter of moments—it is the fear of not being able to get down that has her worried.

3. Children's Park on 9th Street. Fabulous adventure playground. Lots of places to hide. Game of Jet and Star ensues where we are both boys at the mysterious School of Light.

1:00-1:45   Lunch. Mac and cheese, broccoli, milk.

1:45   Read. Current book: Charlie Bone.

3:00   School dismissed.

Christmas in the RV Park

Port Angeles, Washington

December 14, 2009

We are tucked in for the night in an RV park in Port Angeles, Washington, on the Olympic Peninsula. We took the ferry over here today from Seattle. Port Angeles is a town of about 8,000 people across the bay from Victoria, British Columbia.

Our next-door neighbor here at the RV park is a Class A. Judging by the winterizing to the RV it has been here awhile—the wheels are all covered up and a thick canvas skirt is secured around it to help keep the heat inside. It is a fancy rig with two slide-outs. Peeking in the windows, we think it looks like the $250,000 – $400,000 variety. There is a 6-foot, lit-up wreath across the front engine, three spiral Christmas trees of different heights lit up in front of the door, and candles in the window. It looks very cozy. As I was backing up into our space, watching Evan in the rear view window as he was giving me direction, I took a quick sideways glance and caught the eye of the woman inside lighting the candles. We smiled. Hers was a knowing smile. I imagined it to say, "Ahh, the stress of backing up your RV while your husband tells you what to do. Ever since I backed up over Ralph in Idaho and took off, I don't have to listen anymore."

What is her real story?

Maybe she lost the house in the recent recession and is now living in the RV and all these decorations are from her former life that she pulled out of the storage facility. I mean, buying that many decorations for an RV? Where do you store them during the off season? Or maybe she just keeps them up all year. One of "those people"—the kind of folks who never take their lights down and keep their tree up until mid-February.

Is there a pecking order in RV parks? The permanent people vs. those just passing through? The Class A v Class B v Class C v 5th wheels?? You betcha! Here is the run down (according to nobody else but me):

Class A (these are the buses). Usually driven by tiny old men, they are the fanciest of the lineup. Inside they are the equivalent of a one-bedroom apartment in New York. Only roomier and nicer. While they are larger than Class Cs, they are usually occupied by older couples. We have been in many in various showrooms and have even witnessed one with a full-size bathtub and another with a three-foot flat screen TV. Sometimes they even have televisions on the outside so you can sit in your recliner rocker by the lake and watch your favorite Discovery Show at the same time. Talk about weird. Living in an adventure, watching someone else's adventure. And here I am writing about someone having an adventure watching an adventure. WHERE IS REALITY?

Class B (converted camper vans). Think VW bus. Groovy. These are for the serious campers who are either: 1. living out of their camper doing the alternative thing; or 2. mountain climbers who could care less where they sleep (it's cramped in these puppies) but need the room for their gear.

Class C (truck chassis with integrated living—the Big Pig). Families. Most of the rentals are Class Cs as well. Alternative families with websites writing blogs from RV parks in the Pacific Northwest wondering why they think they are so important as to warrant a blog.

5th Wheels. These are the campers that connect into the back of a big pickup truck so that when you get to the RV park you can dismount and drive the truck independently. Hunters. Serious campers.

How I would love to be a sociologist—or more to the point—I just want to ask all the nosey questions that you are never allowed to ask and have a legitimate reason to do it. How I would love to be able to stop the world, find out the answers, and then continue the revolving. In the 7th *Harry Potter* book that we are listening to as we drive, Hermione has just delivered the ever useful forgetful spell ("obliviate"). What I wouldn't give for just a little bit!

Christmas time here in the RV Park. A little sad. We won't be hosting our annual Holiday Party this year, and our ornament collection will be taking the year off. But we have our own bit of cheer going on in the Big Pig. Three nice big red bows adorn the cabinets, two sets of twinkle lights, four matching plastic holiday cups, and a new Santa tea towel that hangs in front of the oven with a matching hand towel in the bathroom.

And we are headed down to my brother and sister-in-law's next week where a proper tree and parties and family await.

Last night we strolled through the town and admired all their decorations in the windows and on the street. When we got back to the RV, we had dinner and then all got in pajamas, lit the fairy lights, added a few tea lights, and started reading aloud from Dickens' *A Christmas Carol*.

No *bah humbug* here, thank you!

Flying Alone with a Walking Stick

Phoenix, AZ

December 22, 2009

I am sitting in the Phoenix Airport on Tuesday the 22nd of December waiting to catch a Southwest flight back to San Jose, CA. Evan and I flew here on Friday to help my mom move into her new place in Scottsdale. We left the kids with my brother and sister-in-law in Palo Alto. That was the tradeoff. They take the boys, we move Mom. Excellent. We are all happy. Evan flew back yesterday, so I am flying alone today. Three nights without my boys after close to four months of rather extreme togetherness has produced interesting separation issues and intrigue around a walking stick.

Alone. Nobody knows I am a mother. Nobody knows I have no set address and that I live in a traveling RV.

On Saturday night I made the mistake of phoning to check in on the boys. Reminder to all mothers whose kids are under the age of 10: Never let them hear your voice if you are away overnight. My sister-in-law Lalitha and I were chatting about their day, how Simon had been feeling, what they had eaten. All was well. "Josh is out on a walk with Garret and the big boys but Simon wants to talk with you," she said. "Great, put him on! Hi, Babe," I said in a bright, sunshine voice. Who knows what Simon was saying between the tears, snorts, and blubbers. My interpretation: "Mommy, I am being tortured by my brother and ignored by everyone else. You are a Bad Mother. I will be scarred for the rest of my life. I will never be able to have a close relationship with any other human being. I will need extreme psychotherapy AND IT IS ALL YOUR FAULT!"

I am at gate C4 in the Phoenix Airport. I am coming home, Sweet Simon!

Lots of families traveling with multicolored backpacks, activity bags, and brothers poking each other. Standing in line at security there was a dad in his late 30s traveling with his three kids. The eldest was about 11 and the dad was getting ready to blow up. "Can't you stop touching or poking your brother for one minute?" he yelled. The answer, of course: "No, I am programmed genetically to be annoying and this won't stop until I am in my early 20s." Which reminds me of the song Simon and I made up last week, sung to the tune of "Up on the Rooftop": "Let's be annoying 1-2-3, I'll poke you and you poke me, Then we will sing an annoying song. If you are lucky it will last REAL L—O—N—G—."

But I am flying by myself. I will not sing the song to the 11-year-old boy behind me. Nobody knows that I am a mother; they would just think I am a weirdo. I am so focused on watching the dad and the three kids I forget to focus on my stuff and make sure the walking stick went through security. It did.

It is a cattle call here at the gate. I am in the C group—the last group. Why even bother figuring out where to position myself. It is just me. Nothing to check in. Nothing to declare. I am flying alone so I can sneak in anywhere. Anonymous. Maybe people are looking at me and thinking I am a business woman typing important documents on my little computer. Maybe they think I am brokering a deal that is worth lots of money and that I am highly valued. But business women don't travel with walking sticks—especially ones painted like green snakes.

Let's be real. Nobody is looking at me. Everyone around me is too busy trying to figure out how to position themselves so that when the flight agent says "GO" they can take off and get the best seat with a roomy overhead compartment.

The gate agents for Southwest Airlines wear regular street clothes. Many are wearing shorts. I don't like that. Call me old-fashioned, but I want my gate agents in a uniform. Not necessarily caps and gloves, but a basic uniform so I can tell them apart from the customers would be nice. For some reason reading Come Caca (written out like Coca-Cola) does not instill deep loyalty or confidence in passengers

There goes the first bell and the masses are off and running onto the plane. Unaccompanied minors are first. Families and the infirmed are next. Maybe I could use the walking stick and pretend I am handicapped so I can go first. But why? So I can sit on the plane longer?

My phone rings. Josh reset my ring tone last week and it is straight out of an Indian Epic Movie. I am thinking of Delhi and I am hungry for a palak paneer. I want to dance with scarves but that would blow my cover as an important business woman with a walking stick. It is Evan. He calls me about every four hours. He is very helpful. He has lots of ideas on how I can be more efficient. I love him. I love the fact that he is always thinking about ways to make my life easier. "Yes, Sweetie, the flight is on time. No, I didn't have any trouble getting the walking stick through security. Yes, I have something to suck on for departure and arrival. See you soon."

Back at Gate C4 . . . oh shit. They just called my name. I was so busy pretending to be an important business woman I forgot to pay attention. They are closing the gate. No problem. Throw my stuff in the bag. It is just me and I am fast. I am at the gate. They check my boarding pass. I am waiting on the gangway at the end of the line behind a mother who looks about 12 holding a beautiful baby. They are both wearing pink velour. We smile. I think she thinks I am old enough to need a walking stick.

I am the last person on the plane. I am entering the cabin. Open seat in the middle of the right-hand second row. I eyeball the woman in the aisle and ask if the seat is free. She moves over to the middle. I put the walking stick on the aisle seat along with my handbag. I shove my carry-on suitcase up above the seat. I spy another overhead for the walking stick. I

Behind the Wheel

sit down. I turn to the woman in the middle and offer to sit there. "No," she says, "just tell me the story of the walking stick."

The Kindness of Strangers
Palo Alto, California

December 30, 2009

For the past three months Simon has been preparing for his 8th birthday. His birthday falls pretty close to Christmas so it can easily be rolled into one big celebration—but not this year, thank you very much. In our household it isn't so much a birth DAY but a birth SEASON.

We started it off the Saturday after Thanksgiving in Hood River, Oregon, with a combined party for Simon and two other adult family members who have birthdays in December. Homemade chocolate cake was on the menu, lots of balloons, party favors, pin the tail on the donkey, musical chairs, and musical statues. Now this may sound rigged, but Simon won all the games! Although to be fair, Grandma, the most sprite-ful octogenarian on the planet, did a phenomenal job dancing to "We Will Rock You" for musical statues. And Grandpa was rudely misinformed when he asked for direction on where to place the donkey's tale and it ended up on the light switch not even in the same room as the donkey.

Leaving Hood River in the rearview mirror, we headed up to Mount St. Helens, then into the big city of Seattle for a few days, across to the Olympic Peninsula, down through the rainforest, back along the Oregon Coast, and on to Highway 5 to Palo Alto.

Every day there was at least one conversation about the upcoming birthday celebrations. More to the point it was a pop quiz to make sure we all knew what was expected on the big day in mid-December.

We were all very well-versed on how Simon would wake up in Aunt Lalitha and Uncle Garret's house on December 17th. Breakfast would be brought to him in bed and would include scrambled eggs, bacon, hot chocolate with extra, extra whipped cream and multicolored sprinkles. He would open one present in the morning and then take the Caltrain from the California Street station up to San Francisco. There would be a walk over to the Powell and Hyde Trolley Car and take it to Fisherman's Wharf, a walk down to Pier 39, an adventure at the aquarium, and then a chance to top it all off at Ghirardelli Square for an ice cream sundae.

Research was done to figure out the train schedule, maps, admission costs for the aquarium, and lists of ice cream flavors available at Ghirardelli.

As the eve of Simon's real birthday approached, Simon was looking more and more pale. Plus he had a nonexistent appetite and a forehead that kept getting warmer and warmer. At 1:00 A.M., an hour in to being eight, he woke up in a feverish stupor saying, "Mom, can I have a raincheck on San Francisco?" His actual birthday was spent at the doctor, but he did rally for a Birthday Bike Ride with Balloons thanks to Miracle Motrin, bubblegum flavored.

On December 28th, 11 days into being eight, we were in San Francisco for the Birthday Makeup Day—and, hang on to your hats, Ladies and Gentlemen—you may wonder if the following could possibly be true, but it is!

A cable car ride. You have to ride the cable car up and down the incredible hills of SF, especially if it is your birthday. But when there is a 90-minute wait behind 548 fellow tourists, you start questioning just how necessary it really is. Who knew that the week between Christmas and New Year's would find San Francisco crammed full with everybody and their mother? The line wrapped around the roundhouse and circled down the long block toward Union Square.

We had been waiting about 15 minutes and had moved up hardly 10 feet. There were plenty of cable cars coming and going, but it takes a while to unload them, turn them around, and load them up again with the maximum of 50 passengers per car. There was a cable car next to us with a couple of conductors in their brown uniforms chatting and laughing. I got to thinking there must be some other stops along the way. So I asked Simon if he would feel comfortable asking the conductor if there was another stop nearby where we could board that didn't have such a crazy line. He said he felt fine asking them, and I reminded him to be polite and wait for them to finish their conversation before he asked. He looked back at me and asked, smiling, "Should I tell the conductor it is my birthday?"

"Sure, why not?" I replied.

Simon waited patiently for the conductors, who spoke in a mixture of English and Spanish, to finish up their chat while I watched from our place in line. The conversation ended. Simon looked up at the conductor and started out, "Excuse me, sir. I am sorry to interrupt but today is my birthday and I was wondering if there might be another line . . ."

The conductor stopped Simon and asked him his name, how old he was, and who he was here with. Then he said, "Come on up here, Simon. Today is your lucky day." Not only did he pull us out of the line to allow the two of us to jump aboard the trolley car, he also held Simon up to ring the bell and instructed us to sit in the very front. Then, after he spun the cable car around on the Round House to get us going in the right direction he shouted, "No other passengers on this trolley car today, folks. This is the Simon Birthday Special."

Should the conductor be suspended for favoritism of adorable eight-year-old red-headed boys? Did Simon work the birthday angle? Perhaps a little of both, but it made for a memory that will last a lifetime.

First Freak-out of the New Year

Santa Monica, California

January 4, 2010

It is 2:34 A.M. in Santa Monica, CA. Never a good time to wake up and think about your life. You will never find the things you like about your life at 2:34 A.M.

We head out in the RV again tomorrow after basically three weeks of indulging our collective selves in all things Christmas, family, and friends. We have been staying in my brother and sister-in-law's lovely house in Palo Alto and now my friend Janet's wonderful home in Santa Monica. We have been showering in proper bathrooms, and we've had laundry facilities at our beck and call. We have been cooking in proper kitchens. We have had friends and family to talk to who love us and remind us that we had lives prior to the RV. Friends and family to play board games with, learn from, share stories with, and plan meals together.

Yesterday Janet, whom I have known since I was seven, and I spent the day at the Korean Massage Palace in downtown L.A. soaking in hot baths filled with detoxifying tea prior to the all-over body loofah and head-to-toe massage. For an hour and a half, an elderly Korean woman, dressed in black underpants and bra—very bizarre!—rubbed me clean of seven months of road warrior knots and calluses and washed my hair with eucalyptus. We never spoke, although she did ask me to turn over once.

The past three weeks have been a much appreciated vacation from our adventure.

But our 29-foot reality is sitting parked in front of the house. I realize I have indulged myself these past few weeks into thinking of the RV as a huge piece of luggage we can drive rather than a home, a lifestyle choice, my reality.

Oh shit. Here we go again. Back into the Big Pig. But these last two months on the road will be different because it is just that. Only two more months. "After seven months of being homeless, two months is a piece of cake," I tell myself. But at 2:34 in the morning it is my neurotic self that takes over.

A list! If I write a list of my issues then all will be written down and I can tackle it all in a systematic way. Virgos love lists. Very organized.

Problem: I drink too much. Solution: Stop drinking.
Problem: I am fat. Solution: Stop eating
Problem: My kids don't eat right. Solution: Give them healthy foods.
Problem: My husband doesn't eat right. Solution: Yell at him.
Problem: Nobody is sleeping enough. Solution: Sleep more.
Problem: We all sleep too much. Solution: Set an alarm.

Behind the Wheel

Problem: We need to find a place to live. Solution: Internet
Problem: We need to find jobs. Solution: Start looking.

This freak-out is different from the ones in September when I was staring at seven months of vast expanses of prairie looming in front of me. I can start to feel my freak-outs as slipping back in to being more pedestrian. More like everyone else. Finding jobs, looking for work, fitting into my clothes. Oh brother. Now I am freaking out that my freak-outs aren't as unique anymore.

A whole new level of freak-out. Too absurd.

Gentle Reader, may I leave you with a thought for the New Year: May it be filled with something to laugh about every day. Even if it is the ridiculousness of your own freak-outs at 2:34 A.M. . . . . make that 2:53 A.M. Goodnight.

Wild Animals, Excitement, and Equipment for Your Bed

Anaheim, California

January 6, 2010

Last month when we were in Seattle, Simon and I went to the Woodland Park Zoo. A most excellent day by all accounts. It was just the two of us so we could really focus on the animals Simon wanted to see and not be distracted by the sibling rivalry that seems to be popping up more and more lately.

We were staying at our friend's house in North Seattle and two buses were involved to get to the zoo. We walked out the door from their house, crossed the street, and presto the first bus pulled up right on time. A 10-minute ride to the transfer station. It was one of those cold but bright and sunny days that makes for beautiful crisp skies, and as we looked between the streets as we went whipping by on the bus, we could see Mount Rainier peeking through. The second bus ride was much longer. Enough time to take off our hats and mittens and read a couple of chapters in the books we brought with us.

After 30 minutes or so we got to the zoo and went right up to the admission booth. One of the cool things about homeschooling in the winter is we can go to places that might normally be wild and crazy on the weekend or in the summer. On a Tuesday morning at 10:00 in early December, we had the place all to ourselves. There was a wonderful indoor play space called the Zoomazium, which had a tree to climb up into (with a slide to come down), a climbing structure that looked like something out of *Swiss Family Robinson*, and a stage for live animal demonstrations. Um, no thanks. Not interested in touching the snake.

But we weren't there for the climbing structure really; we were on a safari to find sloth bears, sun bears, elephants (both Asian and African), red pandas, hippos, flamingos, hawks, snakes, birds, penguins, giraffes, and reindeer.

After a day well spent it was time to head to the much anticipated gift shop. I reminded Simon that with just two weeks until his birthday and three weeks until Christmas he was not allowed to buy anything for himself. Plus, he had limited funds and a long list of family members to shop for. For a good half hour we were up and down the aisles of the deserted gift shop touching everything, expanding wish lists for Santa Claus, and remarking, "Ahh, I have this same stuffed snake in a storage box somewhere."

At one point Simon asked if it was alright if he got Evan and me a combined gift for Christmas. "Would you be sad to share a present?" I assured him Dad and I were used to sharing but all we really wanted was a poem he wrote, or a song he made up, or better yet, a certificate to use at a later date for good behavior in a museum. He assured me that he had found the perfect gift and needed to take a $7.00 withdrawal from the Mommy Wallet, where he keeps a running total of his allowance. But the entire process was really to be top secret. He needed the cash but he needed me to keep well away. "No problem. I will be over in the plastic animal section reclassifying the dinosaurs," I said.

Once the secret purchase was made, hidden in the Woodland Park Zoo recyclable brown paper bag, and shoved discretely into the bottom of the backpack, Simon turned to me and asked, "Can I tell you what it is?"

"No! Absolutely not! I love surprises and as an adult you don't get many, so no, I don't want to know," I replied, louder than I should have.

"Oh, but it is really perfect. I bet you want to know," Simon retorted.

This went on for the 15-minute walk back through the park to the exit nearest the bus stop. Finally, I relented. "Alright, you can give me one small clue."

"Well," said Simon, "it is a piece of equipment for your bed."

I laughed out loud, imagining things that couldn't possibly have been sold at the Seattle Zoo Gift Shop that my seven-year-old son could buy with 7 bucks. Had Simon noticed that Evan and I lacked some essential equipment in the queen-size bed in the RV?

"A pillowcase?" I suggested, to peals of laughter.

"Nope, you will just have to wait. But it is definitely something that is missing from your bed."

Three weeks, the Olympic Peninsula, and the Oregon Coast later, the brown Woodland Park Zoo bag appeared under the tree at my brother and sister-in-law's house in Palo Alto with a bow on it. Evan and I opened the gift together. Simon was absolutely right. How could we have lived for so long without this most essential piece of equipment—a stuffed panda! After 14 years our marital bed is finally fully equipped.

Look What's Hangin´   in the RV
Joshua Tree National Park, California

January 12, 2010

Wall space is limited. Knobs act as picture hooks. Choices continually need to be made about what stays and what goes. Christmas was a tricky one—we ended up mailing a big box of lovely but nonessential gifts we received to my in-laws to hold for us until we have a more permanent domicile.

But we couldn't say good-bye to Simon's 298-piece Thornatus V9 that he got from Santa Claus. For those of you not in the know, a Thornatus V9 is a Bionicle. If that doesn't help, Bionicles are made by Lego and are interlocking pieces of molded plastic that when put together (after the 43 steps) make any assortment of absolutely frightening robots, usually graced with axes, swords, javelins, shields, and bows. For a family that bans guns (real or pretend), it seems beyond explanation that we have pardoned hand-to-hand combat weapons. Their names are as frightening as their piercing eyes and absurd number of plastic parts: Makuta, The Dark Hunters, and Scorpio XV1. The Thornatus V9 made the cut, and it is now in the plastic crate under the couch of the RV.

And then there are our walls. Whatever space Evan and I have shared, from our first apartment together in Cambridge, MA, to the three homes we have owned in Massachusetts, Georgia, and London, and the countless rentals in between, we have put up artwork almost immediately. Even here in our rolling home we have things hanging from the knobs and taped onto the walls. They remind us of friends and family and help make our little house a bit more like a home.

Now presenting: The RV Collection. I like to think of these objects as amulets that are helping us on our journey.

Hanging from a knob in the kitchen is a white felt Guardian Angel made by Anna. This is our Safety and Good Parking Spaces Amulet. Anna and I met back in London at Clown School. *Clown* was the name of the nursery and our three-year olds were in the same class. No, they did not teach the children proper techniques for landing should they find themselves being shot out of a cannon—it was just a regular old North London nursery with a funny name. Anna and I would cross paths twice a day for drop-off and pick-up. Being new to the London Preschool Scene I had no idea I wasn't supposed to talk to anyone. And Anna, a wonderful, chatty, brilliant, radiant woman from Brazil didn't know this either, and so started a friendship that went beyond our sons. She joined my book group, and even after her family's big move out of London and up to Kings Langley she still made it down once a month for our Book Group/Pub Crawls where we discussed just about anything under the sun and sometimes the book.

Anna has not only ground flour to make her own bread, she has made the bricks to build the oven she has cooked the bread in. Yes, she made the felt that she sewed into the angel. When I am whining that I have dirt under my fingernails from three states ago, I think of Anna and how I bet she would think that is cool.

In the cockpit hanging from the rearview mirror is the Obama Rama Odor Eater presented to us by Mary. This is our Good Smells Amulet that ensures burnt dinners, rotting pieces of lost cheese, and other unmentionable smells that come from sharing small spaces with three members of the male sex are quickly eradicated. Mary was my former neighbor and friend in London. She was a fellow expatriot and our kids went to the same school, so we worked together as rebel rousers, shaking things up in the school and on our street. During the 2008 elections we ping-ponged so many emails—about Sarah Palin—we experienced withdrawal once the election was over. Whenever I look in the rearview mirror as I am backing up my 15,000-pound home on wheels I think about Mary, Obama, and how I may have taken this whole "Yes We Can" manifesto a little too personally.

On the knob of the cupboard holding Josh's clothes, directly above the couch, are wind chimes given to Josh by his cousin Dow, who currently lives in Manila. I think of this semi-melodious, light tinkling as our Spirituality Good Omen. I heard them as we were driving through the L.A. traffic along the 405, again on the wild turns through the Grand Tetons, and they were chiming out of control today as we hit the dirt roads in Joshua Tree National Park. While they were a gift to Josh for his birthday, they are a reminder to me of my brother and sister-in-law— Dow's parents—who met when they were in the Peace Corps in Mali, West Africa. Throughout their life together they have lived in San Francisco; Hong Kong; Portland, OR; Washington, DC; Niger; London; and now Manila. They make Evan and I look like amateurs at this moving thing. They may look like wanderers on the outside, but they are the most together and grounded couple/family I know, and hearing the lovely lilt reminds me to take a breath.

And then there is the tangerine-rind mobile from my lovely niece Amy that hangs from an electrical knob in our tiny bedroom in the back of the RV. I think of this as our Whimsical Amulet. She made it for us for Christmas knowing we had limited space. She is a fabulous artist (as well as a yoga instructor and graduate student). She tore the tangerine peels to look like flowers and sewed them with fishing wire interspersed with clear crystal-cut beads onto a piece of wood covered with twine. Amy is the kind of woman who questions the world and enjoys the process of finding the answers. She reminds me to look at things with an eye toward possibilities. Why not drive the extra 10 miles to take that family photo with the Giant Artichoke in Castroville, CA? Why not take a flashlight hike to experience the desert at nighttime?

The other things that are taped to the walls include Simon's point chart, showing our dedication to education and discipline through bribery, as well as various score cards from miniature golf games played across the nation, representing our aspiring commitment to athleticism.

All these amulets remind us that we do have a community of friends and family who are traveling with us and are waiting with open arms as we pull up into their driveways in the Big Pig, share a meal, and use their washers and dryers.

Profound Observations of the Absurdly Obvious

Las Vegas, Nevada

January 12, 2010

. . . or is it absurd observations for the profoundly obvious? From time to time a light bulb will go off in my head and a truism will hit me hard. I have been having these profound/absurd observations since my early 20s and they go like this:

Inherited wealth. This means someone in your family bequeaths you money. This implies someone from your family has money. Usually old money. I will never come from inherited wealth.

The Olympics. Every four years I drag this one out: I will never be in the Olympics. Why this surprises me every four years I have no idea. It is not like I have ever been a competitive athlete, but nevertheless I am surprised. Curling. Perhaps curling is in my future.

Traveling. When I was 20 years old I attended Chiang Mai University and lived with a Thai Buddhist family. I had two weeks off from school and decided to fly to Nepal. My host family thought I was insane. "Why would you go to Nepal; we have everything you need in Chiang Mai," they said. It dawned on me: I was the adventurer. They had never been to Bangkok. By having me live with them, I was their adventure.

Uhuru. For our honeymoon Evan and I climbed Mount Kilimanjaro. It was the most unromantic honeymoon you can imagine, filled with altitude sickness and shared smelly bunkrooms, but an adventure I wouldn't trade. I was lying on a thin cot in Kibo Hut pretending to sleep in anticipation of getting up at midnight for the final assent in order to see the first rays of sun as they hit the continent. I was a little delirious as I was lying there fading in and out of sleep but then it came to me: Uhuru is the name of the tallest peak of Kilimanjaro. It is the Swahili word for *freedom*. And then there is Lieutenant Uhuru, the black woman on the original *Star Trek*! (Ok, so her name was *Uhura,* but work with me here.) Who was half of the first interracial kiss on television. The other half, of course, being Captain Kirk.

Cashmere and Kashmir. Beautiful cashmere scarves come from Kashmir, India. Or do they?

Talking. If you tell people something, they will know it. If you don't tell someone something, they won't. And the lesson: You don't have to tell everybody everything.

British accents. Just because someone has a British accent doesn't mean they are smart.

Today's profound observation: Las Vegas is in the middle of a desert. The Mojave desert. There is no water in the Mojave Desert. Las Vegas is unnatural and unsustainable and will eventually dry up and flake away.

Is this such a bad thing?

A Time Share in Vegas, Anyone?

Las Vegas, Baby!

January 17, 2010

Sometimes your time is worth a lot. Sometimes your time is worth diddly. While we have known the former, the later is definitely where we are now. And it was obvious here in Vegas.

We are staying in Vegas because we got a great deal on a room at the Excalibur Hotel. You know, the knight-themed hotel next to the more luxurious Luxor and Mandalay Bay? Twenty-three bucks a night. Half the cost of an RV park and we will more than double our hangout space, plus a full-size bathroom. How could anyone say no? We are here for three nights in between Joshua Tree National Park and the Grand Canyon. We have been to over 15 national parks and monuments, 23 states, lots of friends and family—it is time to show the kids the seedy underbelly of America.

Right now I am questioning our thinking on that one.

So far we have introduced them to the gambling culture, smoke-filled casino floors, Breakfast of Champions Las Vegas-style (when the man walked past us at 7:30 A.M. with a beer in each hand), one-armed bandits, video arcades, cheap buffets, The Mob, and sexism in a variety of ways from female escort services to scantily dressed women. If you haven't been to Vegas lately, the strip (for those who decide to walk) is chock-a-block with groups of what appear to be newly arrived immigrants from south of the border, dressed in neon-yellow shirts and matching hats all emblazoned with the same motto: *Girls to your door in 20 minutes.* They also hand out the matching business cards with the number to call. How convenient.

In the 13 years since Evan and I were last here, the free Pirate Show in front of the Treasure Island Hotel has gone from showcasing Disney-approved, fresh-faced pirates to pole-dancing, g-string-wearing pirates. Thirteen years ago there was a battle between the British man of war and the pirate ship. Now it's the ship of Sirens (the aforementioned scantily clad women) vs. the Pirates. To add misogynistic insult to injury, when the pirates decide to fire their cannons at the Sirens (how else could the show's directors showcase all the pyrotechnic power designed for the original show?), the Pirates decide to bring the Sirens to submission by "attacking their closets, where it will hurt the most."

I apologized to Josh for taking him to this X-rated show. In a good-natured way he replied, "This will be a good story to tell my friends: *Then there was the time my parents took me to see naked ladies in Vegas . . .*"

Back to the story.

Behind the Wheel

Evan drops the kids and me in front of the Excalibur so we can check-in while he deals with parking the Big Pig in the back parking lot. We walk in the front doors, Josh and I with a rolling bag each and computers in our backpacks. Simon is carrying two bags: one filled with toiletries and the other with the mandatory stuffed animals. In order to check-in you need to take the long stinky walk through the casino. The coolest part about the Excalibur is the outside because you can pretend it is a castle. Inside it is a smoke-filled, darkly lit, loud casino filled with sad, overweight people from all over the world blankly looking at electronic gambling machines as they keep pouring their quarters in, in hopes of what? Capturing the American dream, perhaps.

We make our way along the beer-stained carpet following the overhead signs to Registration. Before we make it there, we are stopped by a smiling woman who asks how long we are here for. Are we planning on seeing a show? "Not for $70 a person we aren't," I quip. "Well, what about for $50 for the four of you to see *The Tournament of Kings* (produced by Peter Jackson, the New Zealander who also did *Lord of the Rings*)?" Now she's talking. What is the catch?

A TIME SHARE PRESENTATION!

Take me back . . . Minneapolis 1984. My first job out of college, I called people out of the phone book for Quadna Mountain Vacation Resort in beautiful Hill City, Minnesota. "Mrs. Svensgaard? You the winner of a five-piece set of luggage. All you have to do is go to a presentation for Quadna Mountain and the luggage is all yours. Free of charge!" The fact that it was called Quadna MOUNTAIN in one of the flattest states in the union should have been a warning.

Las Vegas 2010. No longer are perky 23-year-olds calling people out of the phone book from basements for $5 an hour. Now they are accosting families as they walk into Vegas hotels and offering cheap show tickets. The Grandview is a huge time share multiplex about 2 miles past the end of the strip. All we needed to do was attend the two- to three-hour presentation and fork over $50 cash now and the tickets would be ours. Dinner and theater for $12.50 each. The catch is that both Evan and I have to attend. That is six hours of our combined time. In the old days, when we used to think in billable hours, that time was worth a lot. Now we see our time as an opportunity to save money. We sign up.

We meet the bus at 9:30. We meet our assigned salesman, Rodney, at 10:15. The pitch starts. Wow. He is good. He tells us his story of growing up with a young single mother. His worst day of school every year was the first day when all the kids would stand up and talk about where they had gone on their summer vacations. Who knew so many kids from Hot Springs, Arkansas, had Hawaiian vacations or went to Disneyland? But not Rodney and his sister. They got to know their backyard inside and out. Selling time shares appears to be all about appealing to people's need to ensure that they never have bad vacations again. Bottom line: a two-week time share in Vegas for $39,999. No thanks; we are here for the *Tournament of Kings* tickets.

Then we meet Rick, Rodney's manager. He goes through the numbers with us (and offers us some better deals). Bottom line: Rick starts at $30,000 for two weeks of time share with four bonus weeks thrown in. Rick ends at $15,000 for one week. No thanks; we are here for the tickets.

Then we are sent to the Gift Desk and meet with Robin. She is from Hawaii and gives us some tips for when we are there in a few weeks. She isn't really the Ticket Woman. She tries for a third time to sell us a time share. Bottom line: Every third year for $600. No thanks; tickets please.

Then we meet with Dora. She gives us the tickets.

Back to the hotel room by 1:00 P.M. with tickets in hand.

The show was great. The boys wanted us to sit through another time share presentation so we could see it again the following night.

No thanks. Some things you just can't do, even for your kids.

Tornados, RV Parks, and *City of New Orleans*

Scottsdale, AZ

January 22, 2010

We are in Scottsdale, Arizona, visiting my mom, who has recently moved here after 30 years in San Diego. She moved here because San Diego wasn't hot enough for her, and when you have arthritis, deep penetrating desert warmth is what you would sell your best milking cow—or your condo in San Diego—for.

("Your best milking cow . . ." Where did that farm analogy come from? Clearly I have been spending a little too much time in rural areas and watching reruns of *The Waltons*.)

It has been uncharacteristically cold and rainy since we arrived in Scottsdale, and tonight there is a severe weather warning with the chance of tornados. I have a new relationship with tornados now that we don't have a root cellar to climb down into from the RV. And—let's call it like it is—tornados have homing devices for RVs and trailer parks.

After growing up in Minnesota, I am all too familiar with the sirens that ring out to signal a tornado warning and the importance of getting into the basement ASAP. When I was a kid I would console myself, knowing that we would be safe because we were in the basement and besides, the tornados would go for the trailer parks first. Needless to say I have a different view of the situation now.

At 10:00 P.M. the tornado warning was downgraded to mere Flash Floods so we felt comfortable hitting the road. We packed up the three bags of clean laundry we had done at Mom's place, along with the 14 new books we had checked out from her local public library, which is called, exotically, The Arabian Branch. We bundled Simon up in his spaceman pajamas, loaded Josh down with bags, and headed out in Mom's car to the cheap hotel where we are staying just a 20-minute drive down the freeway. We aren't staying at an RV park because, according to Steve at the OK Corral RV Park, "We booked up months ago 'cause of The Car Show." I was kind of waiting for him to add, "Asshole" to the end of that sentence or at least, "duh." Like I was supposed to know about The Car Show? My question is, "What are RV drivers doing at a CAR show?" Traitors.

So here we are—10:30 on a Thursday night at the Bell Motel located next to the self-storage facility alongside Highway 17 in a torrential rainstorm. Mom's car is parked alongside the Big Pig. As we walked in our room the carpet was all squishy from the rain seeping in under the door.

Simon is having trouble falling asleep because he is scared of tornados, Josh is hiding under the covers playing on his iPod touch, and Evan just disappeared to the hotel office in search of the free popcorn.

In the past three weeks since we left Santa Monica, we have been in Anaheim, Big Bear, Joshua Tree, Kingman, Las Vegas, and the Grand Canyon. I am feeling like a microwaved bag of popcorn myself—we have been bopping around so much.

Simon has just crawled into bed with me, bringing along his three stuffed animals. A bear, a panda, and a turtle. These are the mainstays. The beds change, the cities change, but he still has his spaceman pajamas, his stuffed animals, and the song I sing. His song. *City of New Orleans* by Steve Goodman. I have sung this song to him—yes, all three verses—most every night since he was two. He is now eight. So, 6 years x 365 days = 2190 times singing *City of New Orleans*.

I normally don't hear the words I sing anymore. Tonight I did. Appropriately, a song about travel. 926 miles worth of travel from Chicago to New Orleans. "Mothers with their babes asleep / are rockin' to the gentle beat / and the rhythm of the rails is all they dream." I suppose after seven months on the road we do have a rhythm. Sometimes it is the tapping of the keys on the computer, sometimes it is the packing and repacking, but mostly it is the constant movement. Simon is now asleep lying against me as I type. His steady breathing is a comfort to me just as my singing the same song to him each night no matter where we are is a comfort to him.

"Goodnight America, how are ya? / Don't ya know me, I'm your native son / I'm a train they call The City of New Orleans / I'll be gone five hundred miles when the day is done. "

The Walmart Beauty Salon: A Hairy Experience or Just a Good Deal?

Scottsdale, Arizona

January 30, 2010

I love oxymorons. Jumbo shrimp. Plastic silverware. Just wars. Butthead. Clogged drain.

Before we started the RV trip, who would have thought I would have another to add to this list? Let alone an oxymoron I could actually walk in to. I am talking about the Walmart Beauty Salon.

But first, we need to talk about hair. Let's be real. Does anyone like their hair? Too thin, too thick, too straight, too curly, wrong color. Very few people I have met will honestly say, "Yes, I like my hair." Certainly not me. While other girls would brush their hair for hours, I never had enough mass to keep me busy for more than a minute or two. While other girls would take a hair band and wrap it around their ponytails twice, mine would go around my thin little strands four times and then still fall out. Every hairdresser I've seen since I was 12 has acted like she was giving me new, vital, secret information by telling me in a hushed voice, "Honey, you have thin hair." Well, at least there is one thing thin on my body.

I remember my bald father making a comment to me somewhere in my early teens about my hair and then making the jump to his mother . . . "old cue ball." Great. More fodder for future nightmares: Bald by the age of 20. Luckily, I really don't care. And as a person who is not particularly fussy about her outward appearance and has trouble passing up a swimming opportunity, having my thin hair is, in some ways, a blessing. My hair dries really fast.

Every once in a while, Evan and I have little conversations about how lucky the other one is to have married someone who comes with some obscure special skill that didn't come to light until after the vows were exchanged. Evan, for example, is The Coupon Guru. Whenever we arrive in a new place, which is quite often in the past seven months, he goes through the free newspapers and circulars that are at the front of the local grocery stores that everyone else walks right by. He finds all sorts of 2-for-1 restaurant deals, Internet deals, and special deals for families living in RVs with red-headed boys, bald husbands, and thin-haired wives.

The added bonus that I brought to the marriage is that I don't spend money on my looks. "Just think how much money we have saved over the past 14 years because I am low-maintenance in the beauty department!" I have often quipped to Evan.

Since we have been homeless, I have had my hair cut twice. Once in Dillon, Montana, in late October for $24 by a nice chatty hairdresser named Cheryl, who told me way too much information about her relationship with her husband.

My second haircut was last week in Scottsdale, AZ.

Mom and I had a couple of hours to kill and Mom, as only a mother can, let it be known in her most gentlest of ways that it was time for me to get my hair cut. Yes, my 76-year-old mother still mothers her 47-year-old baby. I guess it never ends.

Off we go to the strip malls of the Happy Valley—just north of North Scottsdale and coming up empty on the Beauty Salon Front. I spy a Sally's Beauty Supply Shop, which I figure might be a good place to do some reconnaissance/information gathering—get some reliable information from natives in the know. I pull up, leave the car running, and jump out. There is a long line at the cash register of relatively coiffed women who I figure are locals. I decide to treat the long line of women as if they have gathered there just for me. I clear my throat and begin, "Excuse me, ladies, I am new to the Scottsdale area and am looking for a place to get my hair cut. Does anyone have a suggestion?" A woman with jet black hair and many boxes of hair products in her basket takes the bait and says, "There is Roxy's across at the mall or Walmart next door. Roxy's is pretty pricey and you need an appointment."

Back in the car I lay out the options to Mom. No choice. We pull into Walmart. I have used Walmart on and off for a lot of things over the past seven months on the road trip. I have slept in their parking lots in Kansas, Wyoming, South Dakota, and North Dakota. I have eaten their food, worn their clothes, and decorated the interior of the RV for Christmas entirely with Walmart products. And now I am about to go under the Walmart knife . . . um, scissors. A new form of Walmart baptism? Is the next step to go to the Walmart Tattoo Parlor and have their logo put upon my arm? Or perhaps go to City Hall and change my name to Wendy Walmart? When does it end?

We enter the beauty salon portion of Walmart. Yes, there are two beauticians available right now. Right next to each other. We are lucky, the woman at the front lets us know. On Saturday at noon there is usually a line out the door. Mom's beautician is male, has a wild black Mohawk, and stinks of cigarettes. My beautician is a chatty Korean woman, and our conversation is mostly about kimchi and how you either love it or hate it.

We emerge 30 minutes later with matching hairdos for $17.95 a piece for a wash, cut, and blow dry. The experience, like my thin hair, is less hairier than expected.

RVers in Paradise

Big Island, Hawaii

February 5, 2010

We made it to Hawaii. I know the locals spell it *Hawai'i* but I find it a bit embarrassing spelling it that way, let alone pronouncing it with a V for the W and a hiccup at the end. Like Americans who speak with fake British accents in London, do they think they are getting away with it? Posers.

Back in September, when I was freaking out about the ominous trip in front of us, I never really thought we would make it to Hawaii. I thought I would be committed long before then. But here we are, RVers in paradise, heaven on earth with a room that is nice. My apologies to Jimmy Buffet.

The Big Pig is taking a vacation in Tempe, AZ, parked in the lot of the Days Inn. While I thought there might be a magic button that would transform the Winnebago Itasca Impulse into a flying contraption—or at least a 29-foot raft—kind of like *The Magic School Bus*, the secret button turned out to be a crossover switch you push in case you run down the engine battery and need to jump it off the house battery. I actually know what that means.

Are we whimps for not renting and RV and touring around Hawaii? It is actually cheaper to rent a car and stay in cheap condo. But anyway, here we are in Punalu'u the Big Island of Hawaii. This truly is a paradise. And as if it needs underlining, Simon found a coconut and we spent a good four hours as a family figuring out how to open it up. Josh finally smashed the bugger with a well-placed lava rock. A lava rock. Doesn't everyone have one hanging around on their lanai?

Where I am sitting: On our lanai. You know you are in an exotic locale when people use the word *lanai* like it is an everyday word. If you call your patio a lanai it ups the resale value—at the risk of making you sound pretentious. But it's ok to call a lanai a lanai when you are this close to the equator.

We have a one-bedroom condo on a golf course right next to the only black sand beach on the island of Hawaii. There is a little framed tile hanging on the outside of the lanai next to the sliding glass door that reads "Mahalo for removing your slippers." *Mahalo* is the Hawaiian word for *thank-you*. *Slippers* is the accepted word for *flip flops*. Flip flops are the Footwear Formerly Known as Thongs. But now *thongs* has an entirely new meaning.

People say the word *mahalo* a lot to tourists in Waikiki on the Island of Oahu, which is where 80 percent of the population lives and most of the tourists visit. I think they are trying to make you feel like you are in the know because they are using a non-English word. They are letting you in on a secret.

But I have noticed, now that we are out of Oahu and on the Island of Hawaii, nobody but white people use the word.

What I am drinking: Vanilla macadamia nut coffee out of a coffee cup with the picture of a hibiscus on it.

What I am wearing: My favorite Laura Ashley summer nightgown with the blue and green flowers my Mom got me a few years ago. 100 percent soft brushed cotton. Modestly (but not particularly stylishly) covered up with a lightweight pink bathrobe I picked up in Holland this past spring. I have worn the bathrobe only three times in the past seven months. I finally feel justified that I brought it because I am wearing it. And my Walmart (God forbid I don't mention Walmart) reading glasses.

What I am looking at: Coconut trees, palm trees, bougainvilleas shaped into bushes that separate our little yard from the golf course. The Pacific Ocean is beyond that and the sun keeps popping out from behind the clouds as I type.

What I hear: So many trilling birds that I don't know the name of. Red-capped sparrows, bright yellow/green parakeets, small mourning doves. And the crashing of the waves.

Where are the boys: Asleep.

What I am thinking: Why the hell can't I relax? Why can't I be one of those women who smiles when she talks and is content to savor the smell of the coffee and the warmth of the sun on her face? Sun on my face! Oh God! I haven't put on sunscreen yet. Skin cancer here I come.

Simon has a cold. Should we really go snorkeling when he has a cold? Kayak out to Captain Cook Monument—a mile-long kayak trip? Sunstroke. Sharks. Mean waves. We will flip over and be trapped underneath and all drown.

I stayed up until 1:00 A.M. finishing the book *Day after Night* by Anita Diamant, the author of *The Red Tent*. Yes, another WWII historical fiction book about women and their plights that I tend to be drawn toward. Then I tossed and turned for another hour, wondering, *Why is it I am so drawn to books about WWII?* Is it because I married a Jew and I want to feel closer to the tribe? Because I have had such an incredible life and I feel guilty that anyone should have such luck and this is the least I can do?

Now I am back to the Do It Yourself Lobotomy Kit idea. If I just had a small lobotomy I could turn off the constant chatter . . . oh, never mind. I am in Hawai'i. Embrace it already. It is a beautiful day. The four of us are together and we are healthy and our biggest decision is do we teach school for a couple of hours before or after we go kayaking.

If I ever have a tile made to hang up on my lanai I want it to read: "It is better to have a bottle in front of me than a frontal lobotomy."

Mahalo for reading this.

Pieces of the Puzzle

New Mexico

February 25, 2010

Simon had a dream last night about a puzzle. Each of us was a different piece of the puzzle. Five pieces in total. The RV was a piece of its own. In his dream the puzzle was breaking apart. Simon's interpretation was that we are all together now but when we finally land in a proper house we will all break apart because we will get too busy in our own individual lives to be together.

Josh thought it meant that it was the RV trip itself that is breaking us apart because we are together too much, don't have our own lives, and are driving each other nuts.

When Evan and I discussed it later—out of earshot of Simon—Evan saw the dream as a fear Simon has of reintegrating into society. He thought it meant that Simon recognizes that we have become closer as a family and likes us all to be near him and available.

I thought it meant he had eaten too close to bedtime.

The dream was a catalyst for a bigger conversation about the trip and if it has brought us closer together or farther apart.

The trip has taught us how to play together, how to trust each other, and how to disagree.

It has taught us that families are made up of individuals and individuals will disagree. But we are a family and we aren't going anywhere so we need to learn how to disagree in a way that isn't hurtful or disrespectful.

It has taught us that we are a family that loves to play board games, have parties, read books, watch *The Waltons,* and swim at water parks. We like stupid jokes, we love and respect our national parks, and we support our public libraries. We enjoy visiting friends and family, and we turn the water off when we brush our teeth.

We are a family that has never liked puzzles.

Small Pleasures

Austin, Texas

February 25, 2010

When you don't have much space, everything is small. Even your pleasures.

This adventure has taught me to notice things again. When you live your life fast and have too much, you forget to see. Or maybe you don't have the time to see.

I still remember the very first pedicure I ever got when I was 34 years old and very pregnant and couldn't see my feet, let alone touch them. That pedicure was heaven. Every pedicure since has been a letdown because it wasn't as needed.

Some of the small pleasures I have let myself indulge in lately are:

- Enjoying the lavender shampoo I bought in Hawaii. I bought the conditioner too. It felt decadent given the tiny budget we are on. It reminds me of walking along Corringham Road in London and teaching Simon how to pull off the flowers, rub then between your hands, and smell. A little bit of heaven in the palm of your hand. Finding the lavender farm where I bought the shampoo was unexpected and beautiful on the hills of Haleakala on the island of Maui.

- Taking an extra couple of minutes in the shower at the Elvis Presley Blvd RV Park shower room to sit in the molded plastic green chair and use a pumice stone.

- Not waking the kids for five minutes so I can sit at the table and write a little bit with a cup of coffee. Coffee—it is all about the ritual. Even on the road.

- Closing the door to the bathroom. When it is the only door in your house, you really notice.

- Walking slowly.

- Looking at myself in the bathroom mirror—really looking.

- Tucking in my eight-year-old baby even though he doesn't need it. Singing him songs even though he doesn't ask for them anymore.

- Sorting through my small jewelry zipper bag of earrings and necklaces I brought with us and remembering the stories of where they all came from.

- Making phone calls to friends instead of emails.

Behind the Wheel

- Lying in the back of the RV, being joined by Josh, and listening to him comment on my aging face, Evan, the world, what he wants to be, and how exciting it is to be 12 years old and have the whole world in front of you.

- Sorting emails by name and thinking about my friends and how lucky I am to have them.

- Rereading emails I wrote 10 years ago. Laughing at my problems that today are barely memories.

It is all about perspective.

Our Own Personal Billgrimage

Little Rock, AK

February 26, 2010

Arkansas is a place you can forget about for months (or even years) and then a whole bunch of references to Arkansas can pop up in an afternoon. For example, in discussing weird laws you might note that it is illegal to keep an alligator in your bathtub in Arkansas, but it is perfectly legal to gather road kill and eat it. As most Southerners note, when they receive an invitation with an RSVP, the *RSVP* stands for *Roasted Squirrel Very Possible.*

There are also a bundle of musical references when it comes to Arkansas. Just think about the great fiddle song *Arkansas Traveler* or, more relevant, Kris Allen, the *American Idol* eighth-season winner, who is from Conway. Then, of course, there is Johnny "The Man in Black" Cash, who was born in Kingsland, and Billy Bob Thornton from Hot Springs. Who knew?

Our Arkansas adventure began when we woke up in Sulphur Springs, Texas, in the Hillcrest Village Mobile Home and RV Park. Our only agenda item was to make it to Hot Springs, Arkansas, that day before the national park closed at 4:00 P.M. Not a far drive. We had some time. We had cruised along Route 30 and crossed the border into Arkansas when we saw an exit sign marked "Hope." Say it with me: "I still believe in a place called Hope." (WJC, 1992 Democratic National Convention, NYC)

We were just passing through Arkansas. We didn't mean to have a religious experience. But I suppose most people who have religious experiences never really plan them. "Hello, God? I would like to book a transformative experience next Tuesday at 2:30 P.M." But since The Holy Bible is the Official State Book of Arkansas, should I be surprised?

William Jefferson Clinton put the state on the map and, as we told our kids, if Clinton hadn't won the election, Evan and I might never have been married. And if we had never married, well . . . they just might want to put down their books and iPods and pay attention as we made our own personal Billgrimage.

Similar to Bill Clinton, Evan and I have our own assorted past. We first met courtesy of the Dukakis/Bentsen Presidential Campaign in 1988 (we came in second) but it was the Clinton Inaugural that clinched the deal. Don't most couples think of their relationships in terms of presidential administrations and campaign cycles? Try it. Every four years take a look at your relationship, give things a shakedown, reelect the good parts, replace the ugly, and rebuild on a stronger foundation. We got married in

Behind the Wheel

1995, and our marriage has been our own personal bridge to the 21st century.

I had nothing to do with the Clinton/Gore 1992 winning campaign. November of 1992 I listened to the election results on a radio in a tea house on Freak Street in Kathmandu, Nepal. Evan, however, was there. Evan was working for McKinsey & Company in NYC, but he volunteered every weekend, flying out wherever he was needed to organize rallies or the now famous bus trip. He spent the final week in Little Rock helping coordinate election day operations from the boiler room.

Given his fabulous organizational and tactical skills, he was asked by the Presidential Inaugural Committee to head up the Opening Ceremonies at the Lincoln Memorial. Evan took a three-month sabbatical from McKinsey to move to DC for the wild ride. In January 1993, Evan hired me, freshly back from Nepal, to head up the 3,000 volunteers. Talk about having Hope.

Fast forward to 2010, on I-30 in the Big Pig. We get off in Hope, Arkansas. We find Clinton's boyhood home. I am behind the wheel and I overshoot the house. I slam on the breaks, Divine intervention. The cars stop. I pull a u-turn in the middle of traffic—hopeful I can do a three-point turn in the midst of an orchestra of honking horns. I hold up traffic for a good five minutes as I slowly drive by the boyhood home of the 42nd President of the United States while Evan snaps pictures. We sigh. It is a fine house. Compared to our RV it is a mansion!

We continue down the street and stop at the Super1Foods in Hope for milk and fresh produce. A bit of Manna from Hope. Evan does the shopping and the boys and I take a walk. Wow. Not a lot of hope going down in Hope. This is a sad town and the boys and I inadvertently find the saddest part. Walking behind the grocery store we cross over the train tracks, past the abandoned houses, and into a neighborhood that looks so forgotten even the residents don't know where they are. After 20 minutes we make our way back to the RV feeling more hopeless than hopeful.

Back on the road, we make it to Hot Springs for the night, and on the next day we head over to Little Rock to the William J Clinton Presidential Library and Museum. Over the past seven months we have been to Abraham Lincoln's home and museum in Springfield, Illinois; Dwight Eisenhower's boyhood home and museum in Abilene, Kansas; and Lyndon Johnson's home in Johnson City, Texas. All those places were about history. The Clinton Library is about our own memories, some shared, some separate.

There are photos of the inauguration fireworks display that Evan signed the contract with the Grucci Brothers for, video clips from the concert Evan organized, the daily schedule from July 12, 1994 when Evan and I were part of the advance team at the Brandenburg Gate in Berlin, t-shirts just like the three I have in our storage facility from AmeriCorps.

Our own Billgrimage reminded me of the incredible Hope we had in 1992 and the excitement I felt for our country. It helped to reenergize me and remind me how one person can make a difference. Yes, the 1990s were full of naïveté and decadence, but there was energy and tingles too. I think about tomorrow (I still don't want to stop) and where our shared nation is headed and I want to be a part of it and to help raise the standard of expectations—starting with myself. I am hearing Michael Jackson singing "Man in the Mirror." I am pledging myself anew.

I am an FOB, and I am proud and full of Hope.

The Big Pig in front of the William J. Clinton Presidential Library

Section IV — Going Home

Declaring Victory and Going Home

Brookline, Massachusetts

March 4, 2010

Any good political organizer knows the importance of finding campaigns that are doable and winnable. And then there are times when you just look around for an easy win in order to give some credibility to the cause and to galvanize the troops to boost their confidence. And then there are times when you just throw in the towel, declare it a win, and go out for a beer.

After 7 months, 28,000 miles, 37 states, and 2,854 gallons of gas, we have decided it is time to put the Big Pig out to pasture and start planning the Victory Party. What a long, strange, wonderful, introspective, eye-opening trip it has been. In these past 7 months we have slept in 33 RV parks, 5 Walmart parking lots, 22 homes of friends and family, 17 hotels, and 2 trains . . . but never at the wheel.

Back in June we were thinking we would get through the entire school year, but the kids are longing to be with other kids, I am longing to be with a larger community that talks more, and Evan is longing to be with people who aren't whining. Although Evan would prefer to be attending Spring training in Florida and teaching math through baseball statistics than digging through our storage facility looking for computer cables so he can connect up the technology to start the job search, even he is appreciating the normalcy of living in an apartment that doesn't move.

Last week we signed a six-month lease on a three-bedroom flat in Brookline, MA. Brookline is known throughout the state for its excellent public schools. Given our long history in Boston and numerous friends on the ground with open arms, it has been a soft landing. The kids have completed a day and a half of school, and initial indications are that Headmasters Penelope Snodgrass and Reginald Higgenbottom from RV Elementary have kept them up to speed!

In the words of Simon, "Mom, our three-bedroom apartment feels like a mansion. Our old house in London must have been a palace." It is all about perspective. Spend seven months in an RV and anyplace is a step up.

I have been amazed at how quickly you can put a life back together. Kind of like a blowup bed. Pull it out of the box, add some hot air, and next thing you know, you are sleeping comfortably. It is wild to think a mere month ago we were flying back from Hawaii and here we are getting ready for the 6th-grade dance and looking at the merits of gerbils vs. hamsters for a pet.

Where is the Big Pig? Comfortably parked on our friend's horse farm in Carlisle, MA. The same horse farm where we were married 14 years ago. We will be cleaning it up to sell it in the next couple of weeks

Over the next couple of months we are both hoping to land meaningful employment in the Boston area, and then buy a house and stay put . . . for awhile. But as our fellow travelers can attest, once a traveler, always a traveler.

Thank you all for your interest in our family's odyssey and support along the way!

Yours in Everlasting Adventure,

Wendy

Conclusion

A Year Later: The Road Signs of Life

Brookline, Massachusetts

March 4, 2011

March Fourth/Forth. I love this day and what it represents. Possibilities.

Here it is—two years from the idea of our adventure and a year since we parked the RV. We have jobs. We bought a house. We have rooms. We have doors. We bathe regularly and buy toilet paper in bulk. I even know where the iron and ironing board are—not that I use them, but I do know where they are. We are stable . . . well, physically anyway. But the trip has changed us, surrounds us, and is with us on an almost daily basis.

Whenever I meet someone and they ask where I moved here from, I first evaluate the situation. If I am meeting them in a work context I say, "London" and leave it at that. If it is a social setting I think about how much time we have, if that person is sitting down, and if I am up for answering the set of questions that will invariably tumble out once I say we moved here from an RV.

The Q & A goes like this:

What was your favorite place?

The real answer: All of them, and for different reasons.

The passenger seat. Staring out at the vast expanse of road and open spaces in Montana. Watching Evan's profile as he drove, with the kids in the back, happily reading.

Crater Lake, Oregon, in November on a snowshoe hike when we stopped to listen to nothing.

The bay in front of the YMCA on Maui where a mother whale and her calf played while my boys ran around and laughed in the gorgeous fields.

My aunt's patio in Jacksonville, Illinois, on an early autumn evening.

Vale, Oregon. A great place to get a piece of pie and a huge conversation with Josh about poverty in America.

The bed in the back of the RV with Simon. Hanging up party lights and making special cuddle caves out of blankets for his stuffed animals.

What was your least favorite place?

The train to Churchill, Manitoba, lying on the seat that turned into a bed of nails. My back still hurts.

Being woken up by drunken teenagers in the Walmart parking lot in North Dakota at 3:00 A.M.

The bed in the back of the RV when Simon was lying next to me sick, again.

How long did it take you to plan?

From the time we had the idea to the time we hit the road—five months. But every day on the road we were changing our plans to meet the new challenges, weather, and moods of the four of us.

Where is the RV now?

We sold the Big Pig and put the money into the mortgage of a regular old house that is not on wheels.

What did you do with all your stuff while you traveled?

A huge climate-controlled storage facility. If you pay in cash, have a lot of stuff, and are looking to rent the facility for a year, you can wheel and deal. Make sure you talk to the manager.

Would you do it again?

Gentle reader, I am here to tell you that yes, I would do it again, but I would do it differently. I would leave out North Dakota. I would go in the summer. I would spend an extra couple of weeks planning. I would travel fewer miles and stay in places longer. I would purchase a larger RV. I would schedule regular Skype sessions with a therapist. But then it would be a different trip. Maybe that can be YOUR trip.

Do your kids still talk to you?

This is the best part. They do. They know we aren't going anywhere and the best way to work out a problem is to keep talking. And if they don't, we threaten to get back in the RV.

Were your kids behind when they went back into the public school?

Not at all. And, quite frankly, they are some of the most interesting kids you will meet. And boy, can they tell some stories!

How did your marriage survive?

I am married to a patient, lovely, creative, brilliant man. The issues that came up on the road were the same issues we had before we got in the RV, only now there were no doors to slam and there was nowhere to hide. Luckily we both have long views on marriage, parenting, and life in general, and so we gave ourselves a lot of room on the small stuff. With all that said—I wouldn't advise an RV trip if you have anything less than a strong marriage.

Was it worth it?

Without a doubt.

Anything you learned from your travels that you would add to your bag?

When Prince Charles was asked what he had learned from all of his travels around the world he replied, "Never pass up a chance to go to the loo." Good advice, but clearly Chuck has never been an adventure traveler. Here are a few things I have learned to add to my bag:

A bathing suit. Lightweight and taking up no more room than a pair of underpants, a bathing suit allows you the freedom to take advantage of that unexpected swimming hole.

A Swiss Army knife (packed in your check-in for air travel of course). Between the corkscrew, tweezers, toothpick, tiny screwdriver for emergency eyeglass repair, and adorable little scissors that can be used in a pinch for a quick trim of the bangs—what is there not to love?

A lightweight scarf. It can be used as a bathing suit cover-up, a shawl, a blanket, a pillow, a diaper, a towel, a picnic cloth, and—for the folic-ly challenged—a hat to keep the sun from doing a number on your bald head.

And a word of advice should you ever decide to travel in an RV: Buy or rent *the largest one you can afford.* Words you will never hear anyone say: "The RV was just too big."

Can you boil it all down to a pithy list of Life's Lessons that can be hung up on a wall?

Funny you should ask.

The Seven Road Signs of Life

1. **Schedule regular tune-ups**. Reevaluate your life from time to time or else years—alright, make that decades—can pass in a flash. At the end of the day, is this the life you wanted or is this the life that happened to you? Stop riding shotgun and climb into the driver's seat already and learn how to reverse that RV around a corner.

2. **Rev up the engine**. Just because you are married and have kids doesn't mean the adventure is over; just incorporate the kids into the adventure.

3. **Dance to the beat of your inner V10 engine**. Society and convention tell us not to take risks, to hold our cards close to our chest, to be prudent decision makers—especially if you have kids! and certainly during an economic downturn. Do you really care about society and convention? It is not so much about courage as it is about trust. It is ok to push the line and take risks and do things differently.

Trust that you are smart enough to be alright, and know that your kids will certainly be fine.

4. **Line up some roadside assistance** Think about your safety nets. Not that you will need them, but they might give you just the amount of confidence and courage you need to make the jump. Although the people who make up your safety net might get jealous and threaten to join you on your adventure, 9 times out of 10 they won't. However, they will certainly want to hear all about your adventure upon your return.

5. **Follow your own roadmap.** You can invent your own family traditions that don't have to be based on what you grew up with. This is the cool part about being a grownup. You get to decide. Wear your pajamas when you drive the RV. Nobody is looking or taking notes that are going down in your mysterious "permanent record." SECRET REVEALED: There is no "permanent record" other than your own memory.

6. **Go after your dream car**. The more you are in tune with yourself and your kids, the deeper the experience will be. There will be less whining and arguing, and a better time will be had by all.

7. **Jumpstart your life**. This is it, ladies and gentlemen. If this is your dream, then make it happen. There is no Owner's Manual for your own life. Make it up. Don't feel you need to ask permission—whom would you ask, anyway?

No one has the answers. We are all making it up as we go along, so here's to my friends! May you spend your life adding adventures into your own storage box of memories.

Statistics

Mileage

Miles driven in RV	16,075
Miles in other cars (rented or borrowed but never stolen)	4,336
Train to Churchill . . . and back	720
Flights to and from Hawaii (the RV was no Magic School Bus)	7,476
TOTAL MILES	**28,607**

Overnights

Nights in campgrounds	47
Nights in hotels/condos	42
Nights in Walmart parking lots	6
Nights at homes of family/friends	99
Nights on trains	2
Nights on plane	1
Sleepless nights	I stopped counting
TOTAL	**197**

Attractions

States and Provinces	37
Indoor water parks	3
Elks in heat	39
National parks	24
Polar bears in the wild	6
Dogsled trips	1
Mini-golf games	4
Different swimming locations	20
Museums visited	23
Public libraries visited	18

Who would have thought . . .

The Waltons episodes watched	11
Photos taken	9,053
Photos posted to Flickr	1,172
Photos taken in front of goofy plaster-cast replicas	23
Oil changes for the Big Pig	4
Days spent skiing	2
Friends and family visited	73
RV accidents by Evan	1
RV accidents by Wendy	1
Computers in the RV	3
Urgent Cares/ERs visited	6
Woken up by drunks	2
Inches Josh grew	4
Teeth lost by Josh and Simon	5
Pounds we all gained	28
Run-ins with the law	0

Top Ten Book Club Conversation Topics

1. In the section entitled "A Travel Addict," (see page 10) Wendy writes:

   Visas, international borders, and malaria tablets. It was incredibly liberating and exciting with a sprinkle of scary thrown in. I love that combination.

   Does that resonate with any one?

2. Upon returning to the U.S., Wendy was surprised by how prevalent Christianity was in daily conversation. If you were to look at the U.S. with fresh eyes, what might you notice? What do you think strikes international visitors upon their arrival in the U.S.?

3. If you were in an RV for seven months, who would you want to be with? What three pairs of shoes would you bring?

4. In the beginning of the book, Wendy talks about following the passions of her children on the trip in the hopes of getting them excited for the upcoming adventure (polar bears and volcanoes). How important are passions? Are there places that you could visit that would help to fan the fires to bring your passions to life?

5. When you see RVs tooling down the highway, what comes to mind? Who do you think is in those RVs?

6. Homeschooling. For or against? Could you do it yourself?

7. If you were going to take some time off, where would you want to go? Would you want to go for a longer time and travel rustic or go for a shorter time and stay in fancier places?

8. Timeshares in Las Vegas or Hawaii or anywhere for that matter. Discuss.

9. Where is your nearest national park? (Plan your next book club meeting there!)

10. In the section entitled "Sunday Night Book Group," (see page 24) Wendy writes a list of all the things she talks about with her book group. Anything else you would add?

CPSIA information can be obtained at www.ICGtesting.com
Printed in the USA
LVOW082206230412

278864LV00002B/44/P